ELIZABETH CADY STANTON

AMERICANS
THE *Spirit* OF A *Nation*

ELIZABETH CADY STANTON

"Woman Knows the Cost of Life"

Deborah Kent

 Enslow Publishers, Inc.
40 Industrial Road
Box 398
Berkeley Heights, NJ 07922
USA

http://www.enslow.com

Library of Congress Cataloging-in-Publication Data

Kent, Deborah.
  Elizabeth Cady Stanton : "woman knows the cost of life" / Deborah Kent.
    p. cm. — (Americans—the spirit of a nation)
  Includes bibliographical references and index.
  Summary: "Examines the life of women's rights pioneer Elizabeth Cady Stanton, including her childhood, her tireless battle for women's suffrage, and her legacy in American history"—Provided by publisher.
    ISBN 978-0-7660-3357-3
    1. Stanton, Elizabeth Cady, 1815–1902. 2. Social reformers—United States—Biography—Juvenile literature. 3. Suffragists—United States—Biography—Juvenile literature. I. Title.
    HQ1413.S67K464 2010
    324.6'23092—dc22
    [B]
                                        2009018377

Printed in the United States of America

112009 Lake Book Manufacturing, Inc., Melrose Park, IL

10 9 8 7 6 5 4 3 2 1

To Our Readers: We have done our best to make sure all Internet Addresses in this book were active and appropriate when we went to press. However, the author and the publisher have no control over and assume no liability for the material available on those Internet sites or on other Web sites they may link to. Any comments or suggestions can be sent by e-mail to comments@enslow.com or to the address on the back cover.

♻ Enslow Publishers, Inc., is committed to printing our books on recycled paper. The paper in every book contains 10% to 30% post-consumer waste (PCW). The cover board on the outside of each book contains 100% PCW. Our goal is to do our part to help young people and the environment too!

Illustration Credits: Enslow Publishers, Inc., p. 110; The Granger Collection, New York, pp. 6, 35, 42, 67, 82; Reproduced with the permission of The Historical Society of the Courts of the State of New York and its Web site: www.courts.state.ny.us/history, p. 20; Courtesy of HM Larson, p. 49; Library of Congress, pp. 3, 8, 12, 14, 16, 28, 30, 32, 37, 44, 46, 59, 60, 63, 65, 72, 75, 84, 87, 90, 92, 106, 107, 109; Library of Congress Manuscript Division, pp. 55, 103; © The Metropolitan Museum of Art / Art Resource, NY, p. 53; Michael Kleinfeld / UPI / Landov, p. 113; National Portrait Gallery, Smithsonian Institution / Art Resource, NY, p. 79; Oberlin College Archives, Oberlin College, p. 98; Photography Collection, Miriam & Ira D. Wallach Division of Art, Prints and Photographs, The New York Public Library, Astor, Lenox and Tilden Foundations, pp. 25, 95; Smithsonian American Art Museum, Washington, DC / Art Resource, NY, p. 40; Special Collections, University of Virginia Library, p. 18.

Cover Illustration: Library of Congress (Portrait of Elizabeth Cady Stanton).

CONTENTS

Elizabeth Cady Stanton speaking to the crowd at the Seneca Falls Convention.

1

A Revolution at Seneca Falls

Early on the morning of July 19, 1848, Elizabeth Cady Stanton climbed into a horse-drawn wagon. The sun shone brightly, and the day promised to be a hot one. As the wagon rumbled over the dusty dirt roads of Seneca Falls, New York, Cady Stanton clutched a folder of papers on her lap. She had worked on those pages for a week, carefully writing and rewriting until every word felt exactly right.

Beside Cady Stanton in the wagon rode her sister Harriet Eaton and Harriet's teenage son, Daniel. No one knows what they discussed on the ride, but surely plans for the day ahead were foremost on their minds. Had anyone paid attention to the notice Cady Stanton placed in the *Seneca Falls Courier* and other local newspapers?

The important notice read:

"WOMAN's RIGHTS CONVENTION. —A Convention to discuss the social, civil, and religious condition and rights of woman, will be held in the Wesleyan Chapel, at Seneca Falls, N.Y., on Wednesday and Thursday, the 19th and 20th of July, current; commencing at 10 o'clock A.M."[1]

As her wagon approached the center of the town, Cady Stanton realized she need not have worried about attendance. The roads were crowded with wagons, carriages, and people on horseback, all heading toward the chapel. Most of the travelers were women. Clearly, word of the convention had carried quickly.

Cady Stanton's notice had sparked keen excitement in Seneca Falls and the surrounding towns. One of the women who read about the upcoming convention was nineteen-year-old Charlotte Woodward of Waterloo. Years later, friends remembered that she "ran from one house to another in her neighborhood, and found other women reading [the notice], some with amusement and incredulity, others with absorbed interest."[2] Charlotte and a band of her friends were

Cady Stanton's notice in the Seneca Falls Courier *helped draw a large crowd to the convention. This photo of Cady Stanton was taken in 1854.*

among the women who gathered in front of the chapel at ten o'clock, eagerly waiting for the day's events to unfold.

Cady Stanton climbed down from her wagon and discovered that the chapel doors were still locked. No one had thought to bring the key! Finally, Daniel Eaton wriggled through a window and opened the doors from the inside. Dozens of women made their way into the chapel. Cady Stanton and her good friend, Mary Ann McClintock, greeted them and ushered them to seats. Cady Stanton was happy and relieved to welcome her longtime friend Lucretia Mott. Mott's husband, James, had been ill for several days, but Mott had assured Cady Stanton that she would appear at the convention. She and James were both at the chapel in time for the opening session.

Mary Ann McClintock and Lucretia Mott were among the women who helped Elizabeth Cady Stanton plan the women's rights convention. The idea had been launched only ten days before, on the afternoon of July 9, when Jane and Richard Hunt of the town of Waterloo held a quiet tea party for a group of female friends. The group included Mott, a well-known lecturer and reformer from Philadelphia, who was visiting her sister in the nearby town of Auburn. Mott and most of the other women at the party belonged to the Society of Friends, or Quakers. They expected to discuss an assortment of problems and divisions that had sprung up at the local Quaker meetings. The only non-Quaker at the tea party was Elizabeth Cady Stanton.

The Society of Friends

The Society of Friends, or Quakers, is a Christian denomination that believes every human being has a direct relationship with God. For this reason, they see all human beings as equal, regardless of sex or race.

At Quaker services, or meetings, any member of the congregation is free to speak when so moved. Quakers oppose all forms of violence, including war. Because they believe in the equality of all human beings, the Quakers strongly opposed the enslavement of African Americans.

Cady Stanton was thrilled by the invitation. The mother of three small boys, she spent most of her time caring for her children and running the household. Her husband, Henry Stanton, a lawyer, was often away on business, leaving Cady Stanton to manage on her own. For the past several months she had been busy day and night nursing her children and several of her household servants through attacks of malaria. "I suffered with mental hunger, which, like an empty stomach, is very depressing," she explained in her autobiography. "Cleanliness, order, the love of the beautiful and artistic, all faded away in the struggle to accomplish what was absolutely necessary from hour to hour. Now I understood, as I never had before, how women could sit down and rest in the midst of general disorder."[3]

Exhausted and careworn though she was, Cady Stanton knew that she was not alone. She recognized that women everywhere endured the same hardships. The problem, she realized, lay in the roles society had allotted to women. Girls had few opportunities to get a higher education. Most of the occupations open to men were closed to women, who were seen chiefly as caregivers, cooks, and housekeepers. It was their duty to keep the home running smoothly for their husbands, who went into the world to do the "real" work.

When Cady Stanton sat down at the tea table in the Hunts' home, she turned the discussion to the problems that plagued women's lives. The others all agreed that women carried more than their share of life's burdens. At one point, Richard Hunt entered the room. After listening for a few minutes to the women's grievances he asked, "Why don't you do something about it?"[4]

If only something could be done—but what might it be? How could they begin to overturn the rules for women that had been followed for thousands of years? Elizabeth Cady Stanton and Lucretia Mott hit upon an idea. Eight years before, when they first met, they had talked about organizing a convention on women's rights. At last it seemed that the time was right.

Suddenly, the simple tea party became an eager planning session. The convention must be held soon, the women concluded, before Mott returned to Philadelphia. Hastily they chose the date and location for a two-day convention. The first day would be set aside for women only. Men would be invited to take part during the second day.

In the days that followed, Cady Stanton and several of the other women set to work on a document they called the Declaration of Sentiments. They modeled it after the American Declaration of Independence of 1776. In the opening, they added a small but crucial change. They amended Thomas Jefferson's famous line, "that all *men* are created equal" by adding the words "and women." This was to change the course of history.

On the Sunday before the convention, Cady Stanton visited Mary Ann McClintock and her three daughters. Together, they polished the Declaration of Sentiments and composed a series of resolutions relating to women's rights. They also sent out invitations to several well-respected social reformers in the area. To their delight, the famous antislavery activist Frederick Douglass agreed to attend.

At eleven o'clock on the morning of July 19, an hour behind schedule, Elizabeth Cady Stanton walked to the front of the chapel and called the convention to order. She had very little experience as a public speaker, so she turned over the platform to Lucretia Mott as soon as she could. Mott encouraged the women in the audience to speak freely, to share their thoughts in the day's discussions. Then Cady Stanton

Mary Ann McClintock, along with her three daughters, helped Cady Stanton complete the Declaration of Sentiments to be read at the Seneca Falls Convention.

read aloud the Declaration of Sentiments: "We hold these truths to be self-evident: that all men *and women* are created equal; that they are endowed by their Creator with certain inalienable rights; that among these are life, liberty, and the pursuit of happiness."[5]

> **"We hold these truths to be self-evident: that all men *and women* are created equal . . ."**

By then the temperature had reached 90 degrees.[6] Ignoring the heat, the women at the gathering launched into a lively discussion and made a number of minor changes to the declaration. Cady Stanton went on to read the eleven resolutions that she and the other organizers had prepared. All of the resolutions were based on the idea of equality of the sexes, and called for women to have all the rights and privileges enjoyed by men. Most important was Resolution 9, which stated, "That it is the duty of the women of this country to secure to themselves their sacred right to the elective franchise"—the right to vote.[7]

On the second day of the convention, the Wesleyan Chapel was packed with spectators, both women and sympathetic men. The seats on the main floor were filled, and some people had to sit upstairs in the gallery. In the audience was thirteen-year-old Mary Bascom. She wrote many years later:

> *The whole scene comes before me as vividly as if it were yesterday. . . . [T]he old chapel with its dusty windows, the gallery on three sides, the wooden benches or pews, and the platform with the desk and communion-table,*

results necessarily from the fact of the identity of the race in capabilities and responsibilities.

Resolved, therefore, That, being invested by the Creator with the same capabilities, and the same consciousness of responsibility for their exercise, it is demonstrably the right and duty of woman, equally with man, to promote every righteous cause, by every righteous means ; and especially in regard to the great subjects of morals and religion, it is self-evidently her right to participate with her brother in teaching them, both in private and in public, by writing and by speaking, by any instrumentalities proper to be used, and in any assemblies proper to be held ; and this being a self-evident truth, growing out of the divinely implanted principles of human nature, any custom or authority adverse to it, whether modern or wearing the hoary sanction of antiquity, is to be regarded as self-evident falsehood, and at war with the interests of mankind.

LUCRETIA MOTT read a humorous article from a newspaper, written by MARTHA C. WRIGHT. After an address by E. W. M'CLINTOCK, the meeting adjourned to 10 o'clock the next morning.

In the evening, LUCRETIA MOTT spoke with her usual eloquence and power to a large and intelligent audience on the subject of Reforms in general.

THURSDAY MORNING.

The Convention assembled at the hour appointed, JAMES MOTT, of Philadelphia, in the Chair. The minutes of the previous day having been read, E. C. STANTON again read the Declaration of Sentiments, which was freely discussed by LUCRETIA MOTT, ANSEL BASCOM, S. E. WOODWORTH, THOMAS and MARY ANN M'CLINTOCK,

FREDERICK DOUGLASS, AMY POST, CATHARINE STEBBINS, and ELIZABETH C. STANTON, and was unanimously adopted, as follows :

DECLARATION OF SENTIMENTS.

When, in the course of human events, it becomes necessary for one portion of the family of man to assume among the people of the earth a position different from that which they have hitherto occupied, but one to which the laws of nature and of nature's God entitle them, a decent respect to the opinions of mankind requires that they should declare the causes that impel them to such a course.

We hold these truths to be self-evident : that all men and women are created equal ; that they are endowed by their Creator with certain inalienable rights ; that among these are life, liberty, and the pursuit of happiness ; that to secure these rights governments are instituted, deriving their just powers from the consent of the governed.— Whenever any form of Government becomes destructive of these ends, it is the right of those who suffer from it to refuse allegiance to it, and to insist upon the institution of a new government, laying its foundation on such principles, and organizing its powers in such form as to them shall seem most likely to effect their safety and happiness. Prudence, indeed, will dictate that governments long established should not be changed for light and transient causes ; and accordingly, all experience hath shown that mankind are more disposed to suffer, while evils are sufferable, than to right themselves by abolishing the forms to which they are accustomed. But when a long train of abuses and usurpations, pursuing invariably the same object, evinces a design to reduce them under absolute despotism, it is their duty to throw off such government, and to provide new guards for their future security. Such has been

The Declaration of Sentiments, specifically Resolution 9, caused quite a stir at the Seneca Falls Convention. These pages came from a Report of the Women's Rights Convention, Held at Seneca Falls, New York, July 19 and 20, 1848.

and the group gathered there; Mrs. Stanton, stout, short, with her merry eye and expression of great good humor; Lucretia Mott, whose presence then as now commanded respect wherever she might be; Mary Ann McClintock, a dignified Quaker matron with four daughters around her.[8]

On Thursday morning, the convention voted unanimously to approve the Declaration of Sentiments and the eleven resolutions. At first, some of the attendees were shocked by Cady Stanton's call for the right to vote. They feared that they might be asking for too much. But in the end, Resolution 9 was approved along with all the others. Sixty-eight women signed the documents. They ranged in age from fourteen-year-old Susan Quinn to eighty-one-year-old Catharine Shaw. Thirty-two men also signed separately, indicating their support.

Historians estimate that some three hundred people took part in the Seneca Falls Convention. It was a relatively small gathering in a small New York town. Nevertheless, Elizabeth Cady Stanton and her fellow organizers had staged a historic event—the world's first women's rights convention. For the first time in the United States, women dared to raise their voices together, protesting injustice and calling for change that would profoundly affect half of the population. As Elizabeth Cady Stanton wrote later, the Seneca Falls Convention started "a rebellion such as the world had never before seen."[9]

Chapter 2

"You Should Have Been a Boy"

When Elizabeth Cady was four years old, one day a family servant led her into the nursery to see her newborn sister Catherine. All day friends and relatives came and went through the house, congratulating Mrs. Cady and cooing over the baby. Yet Elizabeth noticed that her sister's arrival was not altogether a joyous event. "I heard so many friends remark, 'What a pity it is she's a girl!' that I felt a kind of compassion for the little baby," she wrote many years later. "True, our family consisted of five girls and only one boy, but I did not understand at that time that girls were considered an inferior order of beings."[1]

Elizabeth Cady was born on November 12, 1815, into the wealthiest family in Johnstown, New York. Her father, Daniel Cady, was a respected lawyer and judge, and the family lived in the biggest house in town. A visitor described it as "an elegant great house . . . [full of] beautiful things and tasteful environments."[2] The house was so large that it comfortably held Judge Cady and his wife Margaret, their six children, several law students who came to study with the judge, and a large staff of servants. At one point the servants numbered twelve in all, including a cook, a laundress, and four nurses to care for the children.

Margaret Livingston Cady, Elizabeth's mother, came from an old New York family. She was proud of her ancestors, especially her grandfather, a hero of the American Revolution. She was a stern, strong-willed woman. But the hardships of her life wore her down. Five of her eleven children died in infancy or early childhood.

When she was growing up, Elizabeth, often called Lizzie, was the fourth of the six surviving children in the Cady family. She had two older sisters, Tryphena and Harriet, and an older brother, Eleazer. Her two younger sisters, Margaret (Madge) and Catherine (Cate), were her dearest playmates.

The Girl in Red Flannel

A host of rules set the tone of the Cady household. As a small child Elizabeth once exclaimed to her nurse,

Elizabeth and her sisters were expected to learn how to be proper young ladies. They had to be obedient and learn to cook and sew. This 1850 illustration from the magazine Godey's Lady's Book *depicts its interpretation of happiness for a domestic woman.*

"I am so tired of that everlasting no! no! no! At school, at home, everywhere it is no! Even at church all the commandments begin 'Thou shalt not.' I suppose God will say 'no' to all we like in the next world."[3] The children were taught to be courteous and obedient. In the winter, their mother insisted on dressing the girls all alike in red coats, red hoods, red mittens, red stockings, and red flannel dresses with scratchy starched collars. Their clothes were so monotonous that Elizabeth Cady avoided red dresses for the rest of her life.

Like all proper young ladies of their day, the Cady girls were expected to learn to cook, sew, and embroider. They were forbidden to splash in the creek as the boys did. The attic, where the family stored many barrels of hickory nuts, cakes of maple sugar, and costumes left by long-dead relatives, was also off-limits. Nevertheless, Lizzie and her younger sisters seized every chance to enjoy these forbidden delights. They chased each other through the woods, fished and swam in the creek, and sneaked into the attic whenever they could escape their nurses' watchful eyes. "We would crack the nuts, nibble the sharp edges of the maple sugar, . . . whirl the old spinning wheels, dress up in our ancestors' clothes, and take a bird's-eye view of the surrounding country from an enticing [window]," Elizabeth recalled. "This was forbidden ground . . . which only made the little escapades more enjoyable."[4]

Though they had plenty of fun, Lizzie and her sisters lived under the cloud of their strict Scottish Presbyterian religion. Every Sunday they sat through long sermons that warned of damnation and hellfire.

To Lizzie, the devil was a constant presence, always watching and waiting. Sometimes at night she imagined him crouching in the corner of her room, glaring at her through the darkness. She would slip out of bed and sit on the stairs, where the light and voices from the rooms below gave her some small comfort.

Among the servants in the Cady household was an African-American man named Peter Teabout. Unlike the stern Scottish nurses, Peter encouraged the children to turn somersaults, climb trees, and play practical jokes.

Judge Daniel Cady had people come to visit him about their legal problems. Elizabeth learned about the unjust laws women dealt with by listening to her father's meetings.

Lizzie loved him dearly. She remembered watching Peter take Communion alone at church, waiting until the white church members had taken their turn: "He looked like a prince, as, with head erect, he walked up the aisle, . . . and yet so strong was prejudice against color in 1823 that no one would kneel beside him."[5]

Peter Teabout was born into slavery around 1784. He did not gain his freedom until 1827, when New York passed a law that freed all of the remaining enslaved people in the state. Lizzie's beloved friend Peter was a slave, her family's possession, until she was twelve years old.[6] Although she wrote about Peter lovingly in her autobiography, Elizabeth Cady Stanton never mentioned his enslavement.

Often people from Johnstown and the surrounding farms visited the Cady home to consult with Judge Cady about their legal problems. Lizzie liked to listen to these consultations, sitting quietly in her father's study. One day a woman named Flora Campbell arrived in tears. Lizzie was very fond of Flora, who sometimes stopped by with gifts of fresh eggs and butter. She listened as Flora explained her problem. Her father had left her a valuable farm when he died. But without Flora's knowledge, her husband had mortgaged the property. Now the creditors were about to drive the family from the land her father had willed to her.

Lizzie waited eagerly for her father to offer Flora Campbell some hope. Instead, he sighed and explained that there was nothing he could do. According to the law, a woman's property automatically passed into her husband's hands when she married. Her husband could

Unequal Under the Law

In the 1830s and 1840s, New York's laws pertaining to women were much like those in states throughout the country. When a woman married, all of her money, land, and personal goods immediately became the property of her husband. (In 1848, New York passed a law allowing married women to inherit property.) A husband had the right to all of his wife's earnings if she had a job. Married women were not allowed to sign contracts, and women could not serve on juries. If a woman committed a crime in her husband's presence, he was held responsible; he was expected to be his wife's master and to keep her under control. Furthermore, women were entirely excluded from the political process. They could not hold office, and they were not permitted to vote. Therefore, they had no way to change the laws that oppressed them.

use it in any way he chose. Judge Cady took a heavy law book from the shelf and showed Flora the page where the law was written.

Lizzie was outraged. She decided to slip into her father's study when he was out and cut the page with the cruel law from the book. But before she could begin, her father came in. When she told him what she wanted to do, he explained that the laws were made by the state legislature in Albany. She could not change anything by cutting the pages from a book. "When you are grown up, and able to prepare a speech," he told her, "you must go down to Albany and talk to the legislators; tell them all you have seen in this office . . . and, if you can persuade them to pass new laws, the old ones will be a dead letter."[7] Elizabeth never forgot this conversation with her father. It showed her a way to fight for the rights of women.

As Good as Any Boy

When Lizzie was eleven, her twenty-year-old brother Eleazer graduated from Union College in Schenectady, New York. Only a few weeks after he returned home, he fell gravely ill. The family watched helplessly as he grew weaker and more feverish day by day. When he died, solemn church bells tolled across the town.

That night Lizzie found her father in the parlor, sitting beside her brother's coffin. His face was ravaged with grief. Longing to console him, she sat on his knee, and he put his arm around her. After a very long silence he sighed and said, "Oh my daughter, I wish you were a boy!" She threw her arms around him and promised that she would be everything her brother was.[8]

Afterward Lizzie, lying awake, thought about her promise. What could she do to fulfill the dreams that her father had planned for his only son? She decided that she would have to learn to ride horseback like a boy, and to gallop and jump ditches and fences. She must also study Greek, Latin, and mathematics—subjects usually reserved for boys and rarely taught to girls.

The next day Lizzie visited Dr. Simon Hosack, the Presbyterian pastor who lived next-door. She told him she wanted to please her father by learning Greek, and asked him to give her a lesson right away. To her delight, Dr. Hosack agreed. Before breakfast Lizzie learned the Greek alphabet and began to piece out a few words.

As the months passed, Dr. Hosack was thrilled with Lizzie's progress. Her grief-stricken father, however, hardly seemed to notice her achievements. Eventually, she enrolled in the Johnstown Academy. She was the only girl in the advanced course of study, and she enjoyed competing with the boys. After much hard work, she won a prize for her mastery of Greek. She raced home to show the prize to her father. Surely he would praise her and tell her she was as valuable as Eleazer had been.

Lizzie's father listened to her excited chatter and examined her prize, a copy of the New Testament in Greek. "Then," she recalled in her autobiography, "while I stood looking and waiting for him to say something which would show that he recognized the equality of the daughter with the son, he kissed me on the forehead and exclaimed, with a sigh, 'Ah, you should have been a boy!'"[9] Lizzie turned away, hiding her tears of disappointment.

In 1830, when Lizzie was fifteen, she finished her studies at the Academy. Most of her male classmates went on to Union College, where Eleazer had studied. Lizzie was upset to learn that girls were not admitted. In fact, in 1830 no college in the United States accepted female students. Eventually, Judge Cady agreed to let Lizzie attend the Troy Seminary, a boarding school for girls. Lizzie missed the presence of boys in her classes. She felt that it was wrong to isolate girls in all-female schools. However, she admired the school's director, Emma Willard, a widow, who believed that girls should be fully educated. Willard established high academic standards for her pupils.

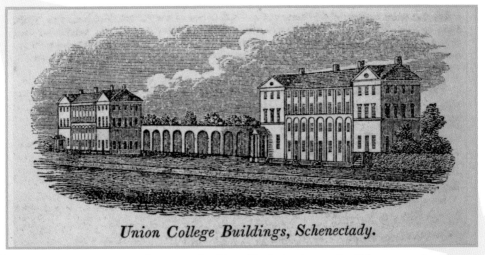

Union College Buildings, Schenectady.

Union College in Schenectady, New York, is shown in this engraving. After finishing her studies at Johnstown Academy, Elizabeth could not go to Union College because the college did not allow women.

At the Troy Seminary, Elizabeth studied algebra, Greek, music, logic, botany, writing, geometry, and modern history.[10] Toward the end of her final term, a fiery preacher named Charles Finney held a six-week revival at the school. A revival is an intensive series of sermons and other activities meant to heighten the religious commitment of those who take part. Finney was a very powerful speaker who convinced his young listeners of their sinfulness. His sermons, which the girls attended every day, vividly described the torments of hell. Years later, Elizabeth remembered Finney as "a terrifier of human souls."[11]

Finney's visions of hellfire filled Elizabeth's mind, rekindling the terrors of her childhood. As the weeks passed, she grew ill in mind and body. When she went home at the end of the school term, her family was frightened by her condition. Her sister Tryphena's husband, Edward Bayard, suggested a trip to Niagara Falls to distract Elizabeth from her gloomy thoughts. During the journey, no one was to speak about religion. Instead, Edward encouraged Elizabeth to read novels and books about science and philosophy. Gradually, her fears faded and she became healthy and happy again. For the rest of her life, she deeply distrusted strict religious teachings.

Henry Stanton, Abolitionist

During her girlhood, Elizabeth and her sisters spent a few weeks every year visiting their cousin Gerrit Smith in the town of Peterboro, New York. In contrast to the stern, solemn Cady household, the Smith home was usually lively and entertaining. Gerrit Smith was both wealthy and generous. He liked to tell his friends, "God gave me money so I could give it away."[12] He was keenly interested in prison reform, the rights of women, temperance (the moderate use of alcohol), and especially the abolition of slavery. The Smiths welcomed guests of every background and belief. Oneida Indians, temperance lecturers, black and white abolitionists, and other family friends gathered around the Smiths' table for food, fellowship, and discussion.

One day, Smith told Elizabeth and her sisters that he wanted to share a secret with them. He led them to a room on the third floor, where they found a beautiful African-American girl named Harriet (not the famous Harriet Tubman). Smith explained that Harriet was fleeing from slavery. That evening he would help her continue her journey to freedom in Canada. He invited Harriet to tell the girls her story. After listening for two hours to Harriet's tale of suffering and humiliation under slavery, Elizabeth became an ardent abolitionist.

Judge Cady heartily disapproved of Elizabeth's fervor for the abolitionist cause. He disapproved of slavery, but he felt that the abolitionists were too radical in their approach. Nevertheless, Elizabeth spent more time in Peterboro. She met famous abolitionists such as William Lloyd Garrison, Wendell Phillips, and a former slave, Frederick Douglass. At every opportunity she attended abolitionist conventions, where men and women spoke passionately about freeing the nation's slaves.

In 1839, when she was twenty-four years old, Elizabeth Cady met Henry B. Stanton, an engaging abolitionist speaker. Stanton had studied theology in Cincinnati, Ohio, but left to work full-time for the cause of abolition. He was a tall, handsome man ten years her senior, and he immediately commanded her attention and respect. Stanton, who often stayed at Gerrit Smith's home, spent more and more time with Elizabeth.

One day, Stanton invited Elizabeth to go with him for an early-morning ride. As they walked their horses along a narrow path, he suddenly turned to her and confessed that he loved her. To Elizabeth's amazement and joy, he asked her to marry him. She answered yes, and they hurried back to the house with their good news.

Elizabeth Cady met Henry Stanton in 1839. Because of pressure from her family, Elizabeth Cady turned down Stanton's first marriage proposal.

To Elizabeth's dismay, Gerrit Smith did not share her excitement. He warned her that Henry Stanton had no means of earning a living. Besides, Judge Cady would never accept an abolitionist as a son-in-law. Despite his talk about women's rights, Smith urged Elizabeth to tell Stanton that marriage was impossible.

Just as her cousin predicted, the match horrified Judge Cady. He told Elizabeth that she must break off her engagement at once. All her life Elizabeth had longed to please her father. She felt she had no choice but to obey him. To her cousin Nancy she wrote sadly, "My engagement with S. is dissolved and I know you wonder and so do I. . . . We are still friends and correspond as before. Perhaps when the storm blows over we may be dearer friends than ever."[13]

Marriage

Henry Stanton was not one to give up easily. In 1840, he wrote to Elizabeth that he planned to attend an international antislavery convention in London. If she would marry him, she could join him on this wonderful adventure.

Elizabeth could not resist this proposal. Throwing aside her father's objections, she married Henry Stanton at last. A Presbyterian minister performed a simple wedding ceremony in Johnstown, with only a few of the couple's friends in attendance. With Stanton in full agreement, she insisted on removing the word "obey" from her wedding vows. A year later, she also determined to keep her maiden name. Instead of being called Mrs. Henry Stanton, as was the custom, she used the name Elizabeth Cady Stanton. From the beginning, she was determined that her marriage to Henry Stanton would be a union between equals.

Forging a Movement

A few weeks after their wedding, Henry and Elizabeth Cady Stanton set off on an eighteen-day voyage to England. The young bride adored the adventure. She asked the sailors endless questions about the workings of the ship. One day, she rode a chair on a pulley to the top of the mast. James Birney, president of the American Antislavery Society, of which Henry Stanton was a delegate, chided her for her unladylike behavior. He even scolded her for calling her husband "Henry" in public. In those days, a proper matron would have called him "Mr. Stanton." Cady Stanton took Birney's criticism good-naturedly. "I was always grateful to anyone who took an interest in my improvement," she explained in her autobiography, "so I laughingly told him, one day, that he . . . might take me squarely in hand and polish me up as speedily as possible."[1]

Nothing could dim Cady Stanton's delight in the wind and waves, and her anticipation of the convention that lay ahead. She looked forward to meeting abolitionist leaders from England, France, and the United States. She was especially eager to meet the delegates from two American women's antislavery organizations.

Behind the Curtain

When the convention opened at Freemason Hall, in London, however, a controversy flared. Many of the male delegates objected to seating the female delegates or allowing them to speak from the convention floor. They quoted Biblical passages, arguing that women should remain in their places and leave action and decision-making to the men. "The clergymen seemed to have God and his angels especially in their care and keeping," Cady Stanton wrote later, "and were in agony lest the women should do or say something to shock the heavenly hosts."[2]

For days, the work of the convention was delayed by the debate over the issue of the female delegates. To Cady Stanton's relief, her husband spoke eloquently on the women's behalf. But, in the end, the female delegates were not allowed to take part in the convention proceedings. All of the women were forced to sit in a curtained-off section of the hall, separated from the men by a railing.

Although many of the male delegates disagreed with this decision, only William Lloyd Garrison acted upon his convictions. "After battling so many long years for the liberties of African slaves," he stated, "I can take no part in a convention that strikes down the most sacred rights of all women."[3] One of the key leaders in the American abolition movement, Garrison refused to participate in the convention, and sat with the women behind the curtain.

William Lloyd Garrison was a leader of the American abolition movement.

After this treatment by the male delegates, the convention had little appeal for Cady Stanton. The truly meaningful aspect of her London visit was her connection with the other women who attended. She formed a special bond with Lucretia Mott. At a time when very few women engaged in public speaking, Mott lectured around the country on abolition, temperance, prison reform, and women's rights. As a Quaker, she held a deeply spiritual belief that all human beings are equal in the eyes of God.

Lucretia Mott, the Quaker Reformer

Born into a Quaker family in Massachusetts, Lucretia Coffin Mott (1793–1880) was raised with the belief that women and men are equal. She and her husband, James Mott, were active in the antislavery movement. They refused to use cotton, sugar, or other goods produced by slave labor. The Motts also sheltered enslaved people who were escaping to freedom. In an age when women were rarely permitted to speak in public, Lucretia Mott lectured widely on the evils of slavery. She organized women's antislavery societies in the United States, and attended the 1840 antislavery convention in London as a delegate. In 1848, she helped Elizabeth Cady Stanton organize the first women's rights convention at Seneca Falls, New York. Throughout her life, Lucretia Mott worked to ensure equal treatment for all people, regardless of race or gender.

In the evenings after the convention sessions, Mott and Cady Stanton talked for hours about the status of women. When their group went sightseeing, Cady Stanton and Mott walked together, lost in their endless discussions. "Wherever our party went," Cady Stanton remembered, "I took possession of Lucretia, much to Henry's vexation."[4] Mott talked to her about Mary Wollstonecraft, an English woman who argued for women's rights nearly fifty years before. She promised to send her a copy of Wollstonecraft's book *Vindication of the Rights of Woman,* published in 1792. The two women decided they would hold a women's rights convention when they returned to the United States. Somehow, they would launch a movement to gain equality for women everywhere.

The Young Matron

After touring for several months in England, Ireland, and France, the Stantons returned to the United States. Henry Stanton had no job, no prospects, and a young wife to support. Though Elizabeth had married against her father's wishes, Judge Cady resolved to make the best of the situation. He accepted his son-in-law as a law clerk. Like many others before him, Stanton became the judge's student. There was plenty of room for the Stantons at the large Cady family home in Johnstown, and they lived there with Elizabeth's parents for nearly two years. When the Cadys moved to Albany in 1842, the Stantons moved with the rest of the household.

In 1841, Benjamin Robert Haydon completed this oil painting of the Antislavery Convention in London. Despite not being able to participate in the convention, Cady Stanton and Lucretia Mott made the most out of their trip to Europe.

Cady Stanton recalled these years with her parents as some of the happiest of her life. She attended abolition and temperance meetings, visited many friends, and kept up a lively correspondence with Lucretia Mott. "The more I think on the present condition of woman, the more I am oppressed with the reality of her degradation," she wrote to Mott in 1841.[5] Yet their plans for a convention on women's rights faded into the background, pushed aside by life's practical demands.

Starting a Family

Cady Stanton's first son, Daniel Cady, was born in Johnstown in 1842, and her second son, Henry, was born in Albany in 1844. Daniel was known in the family as Neil, and young Henry was called Kit. Cady Stanton read everything she could find about child raising. She was appalled by much of the advice in books written by learned physicians. Doctors recommended keeping a baby's head covered with blankets at night and wrapping its body tightly with cloth so that its bones would not become dislocated. Some even suggested giving a baby opium to help it sleep.

For the most part, Cady Stanton ignored the advice she read. She refused to have her babies wrapped, and kept their heads uncovered so they could breathe. She made sure they got plenty of fresh air and sunshine, and they grew healthy and strong. "I trusted neither men nor books absolutely after this," she wrote later, "but continued to use my 'mother's instinct.'"[6]

Happy as she was, Cady Stanton was concerned about money. In 1842, Henry Stanton confided to a friend, "My wife feels very bad, and is sometimes quite gloomy with the apprehension that we shall not get through the coming year."[7] At last, in 1844, Henry Stanton went to Boston to establish a law practice. His wife and children joined him the following year.

Cady Stanton read everything she could about child raising, but decided it was best to follow her "mother's instinct." This daguerreotype shows Cady Stanton with her daughter Harriot in 1856.

> "I put my soul into everything," she remembered in her autobiography, "and hence enjoyed it."

To help them launch their new life, Judge Cady bought the Stantons a house in the Boston suburb of Chelsea. The house had a lovely view of the bay, and Cady Stanton had two servants to assist with child care and household chores. She was thrilled to have a home of her own. Stanton was often away on business, and left the furnishing and decorating in her hands. She delighted in choosing wallpaper, rugs, and tablecloths, and even enjoyed washing clothes, a hot, exhausting task that most homemakers despised. "I put my soul into everything," she remembered in her autobiography, "and hence enjoyed it."[8]

Boston had a thriving community of writers and reformers, and Cady Stanton immediately felt at home. She reconnected with William Lloyd Garrison and Wendell Phillips. She became a devoted admirer of the African-American abolitionist Frederick Douglass and attended his lectures at every opportunity. A visit from her cousin Gerrit Smith was a special treat. Her third son, born in 1845, was named Gerrit and nicknamed Gat.

Though Cady Stanton loved life in Boston, her husband was restless. His law practice did not do well, and he was often ill. He blamed Boston's cold, damp winters, and determined to move to a more favorable climate. He concluded that he would recover his health if he and his family moved to Seneca Falls, New York.

Seneca Falls

Once the decision to move had been made, Henry Stanton encountered one delay after another. In 1847, Cady Stanton went on ahead with the children and worked to ready their new home. In her autobiography she recalled, "My father gave me a check and said, with a smile, 'You believe in woman's capacity to do and dare; now go ahead and put your place in order.'"[9] The house had been empty for years and had fallen into disrepair. Cady Stanton hired carpenters, painters, and gardeners. She scrubbed the floors, hung new curtains, and purchased furniture. But she felt none of the excitement of her housekeeping days in Chelsea. In Seneca Falls, she had few friends, and was isolated with all the household chores and the care of three small boys. Even when her husband finally joined her, he traveled a great deal on business and provided very little support. Cady Stanton recalled:

> *Our residence was on the outskirts of the town, roads [were] very often muddy and no sidewalks most of the way, Mr. Stanton was frequently from home, I had poor servants, and an increasing number of children. To keep a house and grounds in good order, purchase every article for daily use, keep the wardrobes of half a dozen human beings in proper trim, take the children to dentists, shoemakers, and different schools, or find teachers at home, altogether made sufficient work to keep one brain busy, as well as all the hands I could impress into the service.[10]*

Seneca Falls was a prosperous town. The falls that gave the town its name powered mills for grinding wheat into flour and manufacturing wool and cotton textiles. On the outskirts of town were apple orchards, wheat fields, and grazing land for cattle. Instead of paying cash, farmers often bartered for the goods they needed. One local writer described a typical day at the town's general store: "The country customers from far and near would come and rummage over the piles of shoe leather and rattle around among the tinware, . . .

Elizabeth Cady Stanton and her family moved to Seneca Falls in 1847. The falls, which powered the towns manufacturing industries, are shown in this 1850 daguerreotype.

sit round in everybody's way, and go home at night, having had a nice visit, disposing of their eggs at 6 cents a dozen and their butter at 12 cents per pound, with their pay in what they ransacked the store for."[11]

Seneca Falls was not Boston, but reform movements were very much alive there and in the surrounding communities. Temperance societies and antislavery organizations flourished in nearby Waterloo, Auburn, and Rochester. Seneca Falls had a strong temperance following. In 1843, Abby Kelley, a passionate abolitionist, visited Seneca Falls to give a series of lectures. Kelley accused businesses, the government, and most of the churches of supporting slavery. Her fine speeches wakened audiences to the cause. Kelley wrote that Seneca Falls was "stirred to its deepest foundations and henceforth we shall have a permanent foothold here."[12]

Attacked by Kelley and other radical abolitionists, many churches were deeply divided over the slavery issue. Most orthodox Quakers shunned political involvement of any kind. But members of one Quaker group, the Hicksites, felt it their duty to uphold the equality of all human beings. A strong network of Hicksite Quakers worked for abolition in Waterloo and some of the neighboring towns.

A number of antislavery Methodists broke away from their conservative church to form the Wesleyan Methodists. In 1843, they built a chapel in Seneca Falls, the first Wesleyan Methodist church in the United States. It was a plain brick building, forty feet wide by sixty feet long. Its founders dedicated the church to free speech. All speakers except politicians were welcome.

Abby Kelley stirred up the reform movements in Seneca Falls with a series of abolition lectures she gave in 1843. This rare photo shows what is believed to be Abby Kelley (center, wearing a bonnet) at an anti-Fugitive Slave Act convention in Cazenovia, New York. Frederick Douglass is left of Kelley and Cady Stanton's cousin Gerrit Smith is standing behind her.

In most of the reform movements of central New York, women played an increasingly active part. They organized "abolition fairs," selling hand-sewn clothing, hats, quilts, and other goods to raise money for the antislavery societies. Some hid enslaved women and men in their homes on their flight to freedom in

> **"Now men come to antislavery conventions, attracted by the announcement that women are to take part in the deliberations."**

Canada. Some, like Abby Kelley, became abolitionist lecturers. Their work helped to break down long-held objections to women as orators. "A few years ago men in [New York City] hissed at the mere idea of women's speaking in public in [mixed] assemblies," wrote a male abolitionist in 1845. "Now men come to antislavery conventions, attracted by the announcement that women are to take part in the deliberations. . . . Woman is rising up, becoming free."[13]

When Elizabeth Cady Stanton arrived in Seneca Falls in 1847, she had little idea that she had alighted on such fertile ground. But in less than a year, she found a group of women who shared her passion for social justice and were willing to work for the cause of women's rights. With Cady Stanton's gifted leadership, the women's rights movement began at the convention in Seneca Falls.

Chapter 4

"A Caged Lioness"

Three weeks after the Seneca Falls Convention, Elizabeth Cady Stanton attended a second women's rights gathering in Rochester. The conventions stirred a storm of comments in the press. A handful of editorials supported the movement without reservations. In his antislavery paper, *The North Star*, Frederick Douglass noted that "right is of no sex."[1] One editorial described the convention as "the most shocking and unnatural event ever recorded in the history of womanity."[2] The *New York Herald* jeered that the Declaration of

Sentiments had not gone far enough, since it did not demand that women become soldiers and sailors. Horace Greeley, the famous editor of the *New York Tribune,* offered his wary support when he commented, "However unwise and mistaken the demand, it is but the assertion of a natural right and as such must be conceded."[3]

Cady Stanton was surprised by the very hostile responses, but she did not let them discourage her. "Imagine the publicity given to our ideas by thus appearing in a widely circulated sheet like the Herald," she wrote to Lucretia Mott. "It will start women thinking, and men, too, and when men and women think about a new question, the first step in progress is taken. The great fault of mankind is that it will not think."[4]

> **"It will start women thinking, and men, too, and when men and women think about a new question, the first step in progress is taken."**

One of the women who attended the 1848 convention was Amelia Jenks Bloomer, who ran the post office in Seneca Falls. An ardent believer in the temperance cause, she established a newspaper called *The Lily* in 1849. At first, *The Lily* focused on temperance and encouraged women to guide their husbands and sons away from the evils of drink. However, Bloomer realized that without the right to vote or hold office, women could do little to change the laws regarding the sale of alcohol. Eventually, Cady Stanton began to write articles for *The Lily,* and, under her influence, the paper took a strong stand for women's suffrage.

The Bloomer Experiment

One day in the winter of 1851, Cady Stanton's cousin Libby Smith Miller (Gerrit Smith's daughter) arrived in Seneca Falls wearing a remarkable outfit. Instead of the long heavy skirts and layers of petticoats that fashion required for women, she wore a pair of loosely-fitting trousers under a simple knee-length skirt. Cady Stanton was delighted with the new outfit, which Miller had designed herself. She immediately began to wear it at home and in public. In *The Lily,* Cady Stanton and Amelia Bloomer pointed out that women endured great discomfort and even weakened their health by wearing conventional dress, mostly to please men. They urged women to adopt the new style, which was soon known as the "bloomer dress."

For Cady Stanton, the bloomer dress offered exhilarating liberation. "Like a captive set free from his ball and chain, I was always ready for a brisk walk through sleet and snow and rain, to climb a mountain, jump over a fence, work in the garden," she wrote in her autobiography.[5] But the public was outraged by the new design. Boys chased the bloomer-clad women through the streets, calling them names and throwing

The bloomer outfit, named after Amelia Bloomer, offered women a much more comfortable style of clothing. Cady Stanton often wore the new outfit.

stones. Cady Stanton's own sons, ten-year-old Neil and eight-year-old Kit, did not want to be seen with her. Editorials claimed that women's rights advocates wanted to steal their husbands' power by "wearing the pants."

After two years, Cady Stanton gave up wearing the bloomer dress in public and went back to her heavy skirts and petticoats. The bloomer experiment taught her a painful lesson. If she wanted the public to take women's rights seriously, she must appear feminine. She must represent the womanly virtues of caring for home and children while at the same time holding firm to her demand for equal rights.

Tending the Home Fires

After the Seneca Falls Convention, women's rights activists held conventions nearly every year. Usually, Cady Stanton sent a letter to be read from the podium, but she never attended in person. Her endless family responsibilities tied her to the house in Seneca Falls. In her words, the boys were "miserable little underdeveloped vandals."[6] They came home with cuts, scrapes, and black eyes from fights with other children. One day Kit invented a raft made of cork, and tested it on his baby brother Theodore (born in 1851) by floating him down the river. Cady Stanton rescued the baby and told Kit never to put Theodore in the water again. The next day she found that Kit had perched Theo on the roof.

Help came at last when Cady Stanton hired a gentle Quaker woman, Amelia Willard, to be her housekeeper. Willard stayed with the Stanton family for thirty years.

Her steady, caring presence reined in the chaos that was always on the brink of erupting. Theodore Stanton remembered Willard as his mother's "maid, cook, nurse, serving woman, housekeeper, and confidante."[7]

A Partner for Life

One spring evening in 1851, Elizabeth Cady Stanton managed to leave the children for a few hours to attend an antislavery lecture by William Lloyd Garrison, who was touring across New York. On the way home, Amelia Bloomer introduced her to a friend who was visiting from out of town. The visitor was a schoolteacher from Rochester, five years younger than Cady Stanton. Her name was Susan B. Anthony. "There she stood, with her good, earnest face and genial smile, . . . the perfection of neatness and sobriety," Cady Stanton wrote many years later. "I liked her thoroughly, and why I did not at once invite her home with me to dinner, I do not know."[8] Decades later, Anthony and Cady Stanton still joked about this lapse, which Cady Stanton said was due to her worries about the mischief her boys had probably caused in her absence.

In the months after that brief meeting, the two women began to exchange letters. Anthony had grown up in a Quaker family, and from early childhood had been taught to think for herself. She had devoted her energy to the temperance movement, but her exchanges with Cady Stanton quickly won her to the cause of women's suffrage as well. In January 1852, Anthony attended a temperance convention in Rochester, but was not allowed to speak because she was a woman. Furious, she formed the Women's New York State Temperance Society, and Cady Stanton was elected its first president. Cady Stanton used her new position to promote her ideas about women's equality. She pointed out the unfairness of divorce laws enacted by men. At one temperance meeting she declared, "Let no woman remain in the relation of wife with a confirmed drunkard. Let no drunkard be the father of her children."[9]

Such strong statements offended both male and female members. Cady Stanton was voted out of office the following year. With her usual optimism, she was untroubled by her defeat. "Now, Susan, I beg of you to let the past be past, and to waste no powder on the

This bronze statue in Seneca Falls memorializes the first meeting between Cady Stanton and Susan B. Anthony. Amelia Bloomer (center) introduced Cady Stanton and Anthony in the spring of 1851.

Woman's State Temperance Society," she wrote. "We have other and bigger fish to fry."[10]

As a childless, unmarried woman, Susan B. Anthony enjoyed a degree of freedom that Cady Stanton could scarcely imagine. She often attended temperance and women's rights conventions, and traveled from town to town circulating tracts and petitions. She had extraordinary energy and organizing ability. Yet she lacked Cady Stanton's skill as a writer and her ability to draw persuasive arguments from literature and the law. During the 1850s, the two women merged their talents and became an unstoppable team committed to women's suffrage.

Susan B. Anthony became a regular guest at the Stanton home. By looking after the children and helping in the kitchen, she made sure Cady Stanton had time to think and write. Henry Stanton commented that Susan stirs the puddings, Elizabeth stirs up Susan, and Susan "stirs up the world."[11]

> **Susan stirs the puddings, Elizabeth stirs up Susan, and Susan "stirs up the world."**

With her experience as a teacher, Anthony was used to boys' mischief. She usually interrupted the Stanton children's plans before any damage occurred. The boys became convinced that "Aunt Susan" could see around corners.

When they weren't chasing after children, the two friends sat together and lost themselves in deep discussions. One of the Stanton boys recalled years later "the tableau of Mother and Susan seated by a large table covered with books and papers, always talking about the Constitution."[12]

Elizabeth Cady Stanton loved to entertain, and her home became a gathering place for abolitionists, temperance leaders, and women's rights advocates. Women's rights pioneers Lucy Stone, Antoinette Brown, and Harriot Hunt were frequent visitors. Martha Wright and her sister Lucretia Mott sometimes came to call, as did Senator William Seward and his wife. Guests could always count on an evening of delicious food and lively conversation.

Susan B. Anthony, "Aunt Susan"

Susan Brownell Anthony (1820–1906) grew up in a Quaker family in New York State. For several years she taught school while she worked in the temperance and antislavery movements. Her life changed when she met Elizabeth Cady Stanton in 1851. Under Cady Stanton's influence, Anthony became a dedicated crusader in the cause for women's suffrage. For more than fifty years, Anthony and Cady Stanton were close friends and working partners. Anthony handled the arrangements for conventions and lectures, while Cady Stanton wrote articles and speeches. Often, Anthony delivered speeches that Cady Stanton had written. Anthony was loved and respected by the younger women who joined the suffrage movement. She referred to them as her nieces, and they affectionately called her Aunt Susan.

Cady Stanton had a high tolerance for most boyish misbehavior, but she was dismayed when her sons picked up the habit of swearing. When they failed to clean up their language after several warnings, Lucretia Mott suggested a plan. That night at dinner, Mott asked sweetly, in her gentle Quaker speech, "May I give thee some of this damned chicken?" The boys stared at her in shock. During the meal Mott, Anthony, and Cady Stanton swore at every opportunity. They kept it up for the next three or four evenings, always whispering their plan ahead of time to their guests. At last, after the women used spicy language through a dinner with Gerrit Smith and Senator Seward, the boys came to their mother in tears. "What will the Senator and Cousin Gerrit think of you, swearing like that!" they cried.

"Well, you boys do it, and so we thought we would. Don't you like to hear us?" their mother asked. The boys protested that they did not like it at all. "Very well then," Cady Stanton said. "If you boys stop, I will also."[13] After that, the boys spoke at dinner like gentlemen.

A Voice for All

Elizabeth Cady Stanton's family continued to grow. In 1852, she gave birth to her fifth child, a daughter, named Margaret after her grandmother. She was overjoyed to have a girl at last, and flew a white flag to announce her good news to the neighbors.

In 1854, Anthony and other organizers planned to hold a women's rights convention in Albany, New York's state capital. They decided to take their concerns directly to the state legislature, and asked Cady Stanton to be their speaker. With Anthony at the house to keep the children quiet, Cady Stanton set to work preparing her speech. Long ago, her father had encouraged her to speak to the legislature about women's rights. But now, when he learned that his daughter intended to act on that childhood dream, he was so angry that he threatened to cut her out of his will. But, in February 1854, Cady Stanton left the children with Amelia Willard and set out for Albany.

In her autobiography, Cady Stanton described how she stopped in Johnstown to visit her parents on her way to the capital. After dinner, she followed her father into his study and read him the speech she had written with such care. Never before had she felt such fear before an audience, "an audience of one, and that the one of all others whose approbation I most desired, whose disapproval I most feared."[14] When she looked up from her pages at last, she saw tears glistening in her father's eyes. "Surely you have had a happy, comfortable life, with all your wants and needs supplied," her father said. "How can a young woman, tenderly brought up, who has had no bitter personal experience, feel so keenly the

This daguerreotype of Susan B. Anthony was taken around 1850.

wrongs of her sex? Where did you learn this lesson?"[15] Cady Stanton reminded him of the days when she sat in his study, listening to the sad stories of the women who came to him for legal advice. Then, to her great pleasure, her father lifted several law books from the shelves and showed her how to make her speech even better. They worked together until one o'clock in the morning.

Cady Stanton delivered her address before the New York State Legislature on February 14, 1854. She spoke of the laws that allowed husbands to claim their wives' earnings, and granted men custody of their children in cases of divorce. She pointed out that women did not have the most basic rights of citizenship—they could not vote, hold office, or serve on juries. Yet they were required to obey laws created by men. How, she asked, could the lawmakers treat their own mothers, wives, and daughters with such contempt? Several months later, Samuel G. Foote, chairman of the House Judiciary Committee, responded, "The ladies always have the best place and choicest tid-bit at the table. They have the best seats on the carts, carriages and sleighs. . . . If there is any inequality or oppression in the case, the gentlemen are the sufferers."[16]

The Brink of War

With the birth of her second daughter, Harriot (Hattie), in 1856, Cady Stanton felt more than ever overwhelmed by her responsibilities at home. She loved all of her children dearly, but she chafed under the

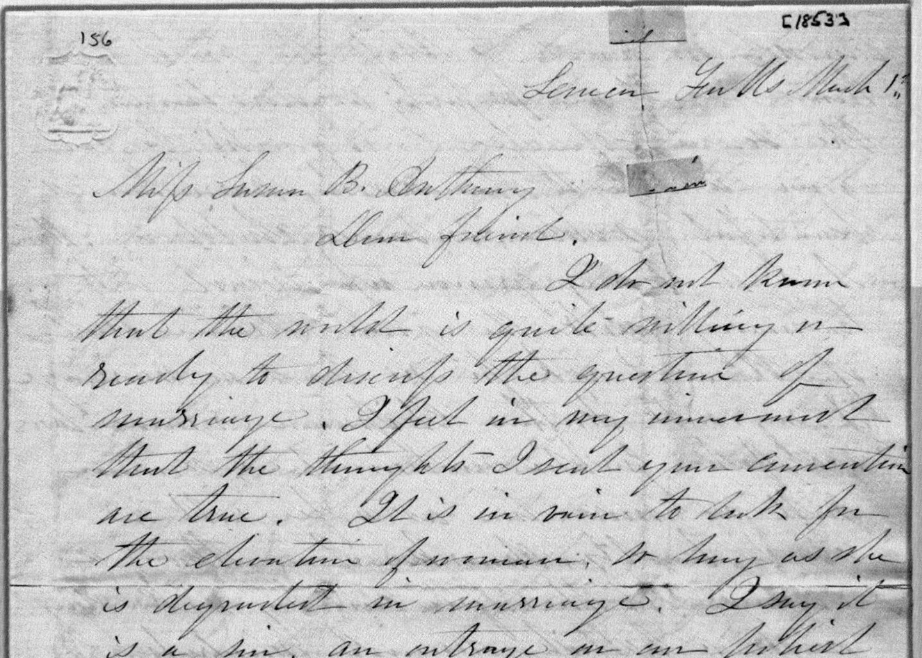
156 [1853]

Seneca Falls March 1st

Miss Susan B. Anthony
Dear friend,
I do not know that the world is quite willing or ready to discuss the question of marriage. I feel in my innermost that the thoughts I sent your convention are true. It is in vain to look for the elevation of woman, so long as she is degraded in marriage. I say it is a sin, an outrage on our holiest feelings to pretend that anything but deep, fervent love & sympathy constitutes marriage. The right idea of marriage is at the foundation of all reforms. How strange it is, man will apply all the improvements in the arts & sciences to everything about him animate & inanimate, but himself. A child conceived in the midst of hate, sin, & discord, nurtured in abuse & injustice

Elizabeth Cady Stanton and Susan B. Anthony frequently exchanged letters. Cady Stanton wrote this letter to Anthony on March 1, 1853.

restrictions of endless child care. "Imagine me, day in and day out, watching, bathing, dressing, nursing, and promenading the precious contents of a little crib in the corner of the room," she wrote to Anthony. "I pace up and down these two chambers of mine like a caged lioness, longing to bring to a close nursing and house-keeping cares. I have other work on hand too."[17]

To make matters worse, her husband resented her controversial stand on women's rights. As he scrambled for a position in the newly formed Republican Party, her demand for women's suffrage and her call for the reform of divorce laws embarrassed him. Cady Stanton wrote to Anthony, "Henry sides with my friends, who oppose me in all that is dearest to my heart. They are not willing that I should write even on the woman question. But I will both write and speak. I wish you to consider this letter strictly confidential. Sometimes, Susan, I struggle in deep waters."[18] In 1858, during one of Henry's brief visits home, she wrote:

> "I wish you to consider this letter strictly confidential. Sometimes, Susan, I struggle in deep waters."

"My dear Susan. . . . How rebellious it makes me feel when I see Henry going about where and how he pleases. He can walk at will through the whole wide world or shut himself up alone, if he pleases, within four walls. As I contrast his freedom with my bondage . . .

I am fired anew and long to pour forth from my own experience the whole long story of woman's wrongs."[19]

She consoled herself with the thought that when her children grew up she would be free at last to devote her full energy to women's rights. "You and I have the prospect of a good long life," she wrote to Anthony. "We shall not be in our prime before fifty, and after that we shall be good for twenty years at least."[20]

At the same time, Cady Stanton supported her husband's involvement with the Republican Party. Established in 1854, the party strongly opposed the spread of slavery into U.S. territories and new states. Cady Stanton wrote to Anthony, "I am rejoiced to say that Henry is heart and soul in the Republican movement and is faithfully stumping the state once more."[21]

In 1859, at the age of forty-three, Cady Stanton gave birth to her last child, Robert. She was left weak and depressed for months. To make matters worse, her father died. She had sought his approval her entire life. Despite his help with her speech before the legislature, she knew that to the end he had grave qualms about her women's rights work. Shortly before his death, she wrote to Anthony that her father still wished she had been a boy.

While Cady Stanton remained in Seneca Falls, Susan B. Anthony traveled the country as a lecturer for the American Anti-Slavery Society (AASS). Tension over the slavery issue was building to a breaking point. In 1859, John Brown, a fiery abolitionist, raided a federal arsenal at Harpers Ferry, Virginia, in an attempt to launch a slave uprising. Brown was arrested and hanged. Gerrit Smith, who had helped to fund Brown's efforts, spent several months in an insane asylum after Brown's death. Cady Stanton, who loved her cousin Gerrit dearly, was deeply saddened by these events.

By the following year, however, Cady Stanton's usual energy and optimism returned. For the first time in several years she made a public appearance, delivering a speech at a convention of the AASS. Her words rang with the intensity of her belief in equal rights for all people, and the high cost that is exacted when any group abuses another. She declared:

> *In settling the question of the negro's rights, we find out the exact limits of our own, for rights never clash or interfere; and where no individual in a community is denied his rights, the mass are the more perfectly protected in theirs; for whenever any class is subject to fraud or injustice, it shows that the spirit of tyranny is at work, and no one can tell where or how or when the infection will spread.*[22]

Within a year, the spread of that infection led the nation into a terrible civil war.

Chapter
5

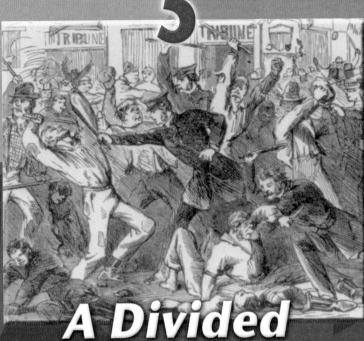

A Divided Sisterhood

arly in 1861, Elizabeth Cady Stanton and Susan B. Anthony set out on an antislavery speaking tour across central New York. Although slavery had been outlawed in New York since 1827, many parts of the state were hostile to the idea of complete and immediate abolition. Henry Stanton urged his wife to stay at home. "I think you risk your lives," he wrote to her from Washington. "[T]he mobocrats would as soon kill you as not. . . . Stand out of the way & let the current run."[1] Undaunted, Anthony and

Cady Stanton carried on with their plans. In Lockport, Rochester, and Elmira, mobs of hecklers shouted them down. In Albany, the mayor headed off violence by sitting beside them on the podium, a rifle resting across his knees. Although he was not an abolitionist, the mayor was determined to protect the women's freedom of speech.

By April 1861, eleven southern states had seceded from the Union to form a new country, the Confederate States of America. On April 12, Confederate troops fired on Union-held Fort Sumter in the harbor at Charleston, South Carolina. The divided nation erupted into civil war.

With the outbreak of war, attention focused on supporting the Union and aiding the troops. Elizabeth Cady Stanton argued that the annual women's rights convention should not be held until the war was over. She believed that the women of the Union should show their patriotism by devoting themselves to their country during this time of crisis. After the war was over, the right to vote would be their just reward.

Susan B. Anthony was aghast at the notion of suspending the women's rights convention. She feared that women would lose the ground they had gained unless they remained active and vigilant. However, nearly all of the convention organizers agreed

A Harper's Weekly illustration shows a woman sewing a soldier's cap. Many women joined the war effort during the Civil War.

with Cady Stanton. While the war raged, no women's rights conventions took place.

A Move to the City

The war brought a major change for the Stanton family. As a dedicated supporter of the Republican Party, Henry Stanton was appointed to be head of the customs house in New York City. He was responsible for insuring that smugglers did not bring illegal goods into the city, and that no goods were shipped to or from the Confederacy. After nearly sixteen years in Seneca Falls, the Stantons sold their home there and moved to New York City—first to Brooklyn and later to Manhattan. Wherever they lived, they always had a room ready for Susan B. Anthony's frequent visits.

From the beginning, Elizabeth Cady Stanton felt at home in New York. The city provided all the excitement she had found in Boston years before. She attended lectures and meetings and cultivated a lively circle of friends. The younger children roller-skated on the city sidewalks and played at a gymnasium near their new home. Neil, the Stantons' oldest son, took a job as clerk at the customs house. Kit, who was only seventeen, ran away and enlisted in the Union Army.

Unfortunately, Henry Stanton disliked his work at the customs house. He was often absent, preferring antislavery meetings to paperwork. Then, early in 1863, it was discovered that the documents related to several shipments had gone missing. A thorough investigation revealed that Neil Stanton had taken a bribe and forged his father's signature on a series of papers. Neil was not prosecuted, but he was fired from his job. The newspapers bristled with rumors that Henry Stanton had been directly involved in the scandal. Within a few months, he was forced to resign. Eventually, he became a reporter for Horace Greeley's *New York Tribune.* He enjoyed newspaper work and pursued it for the rest of his life.

A League of Loyal Women

Northern women threw themselves into the war effort. They knitted socks, made bandages, and served as nurses in army hospitals. On the homefront, they tended farms and ran businesses while the men were away. Cady Stanton and Anthony wanted women to become involved in the political arena as well.

On January 1, 1863, President Lincoln signed the Emancipation Proclamation, freeing all of the enslaved African Americans in the states that had seceded. However, slavery still persisted in several of the states that remained within the Union, including Missouri, Kentucky, Maryland, and Delaware. In May 1863, Elizabeth Cady Stanton founded the National Woman's Loyal League to press for a constitutional amendment that would bring all slavery to an end forever. Cady Stanton hoped to combine the antislavery effort with a renewed thrust for women's rights. At the League's first meeting she proposed a resolution, which stated, "There never can be a true peace in this republic until the civil and political rights of all citizens of African descent and all women are practically established."[2] The resolution passed, but the needs of women were largely overshadowed by the antislavery struggle. Women went from town to town and house to house, collecting signatures on petitions calling for an end to slavery through a Thirteenth Amendment. Eventually, they presented Congress with petitions bearing four hundred thousand names.

The war came frighteningly close to home in the summer of 1863. A series of violent upheavals known as the New York Draft Riots broke out on the streets of Manhattan. In part, the trouble sprang up between Irish immigrants and African Americans, who found themselves competing for the same jobs on the city's docks. Resentment over the military draft was another factor. African Americans and their supporters were blamed for the war and all the pain it caused. Only a

The New York Draft Riots broke out in Manhattan in 1863. An orphanage for African-American children was set on fire only a block from the Stantons' apartment.

block from the Stantons' apartment a mob set fire to an orphanage for African-American children. Since their abolitionist leanings were well-known, the Stantons feared that they might be attacked. After three days of bloodshed, police and military units restored order in the city.

Betrayal and Outrage

Finally, in April 1865, the last shots of the Civil War were fired. A Union victory reunited the nation. The Thirteenth Amendment to the U.S. Constitution ended slavery everywhere, but the newly freed African Americans still lacked the full rights of citizenship.

In 1866, Lucretia Mott was elected president of the newly formed American Equal Rights Association (AERA). Cady Stanton and Susan B. Anthony were members of the executive board. The AERA was committed to work for universal suffrage—voting rights for both African Americans and women. However, it soon became clear that for most reformers the rights of African-American males took precedence over the rights of women of either race. "I say, 'One question at a time,'" declared Wendell Phillips. "This is the negro's hour."[3] African Americans had suffered unthinkable misery under slavery. A single-minded effort was needed to secure their voting rights. Lucy Stone and many other supporters of women's suffrage echoed Phillips' sentiments. They insisted that voting rights for African-American men must come first. Women's needs were less pressing. Women could wait their turn.

Cady Stanton had worked for women's suffrage since 1848. She was convinced that unless women gained equal rights in 1866, they might have to wait for decades. In dismay, she watched her old allies turn their backs on women's suffrage. Wendell Phillips, Lucy Stone, Horace Greeley, William Lloyd Garrison, Frederick Douglass, and even her beloved cousin Gerrit Smith, argued in favor of voting rights for black men only. "I have argued constantly with the whole fraternity, but I fear one and all will favor enfranchising the negro without us," she wrote to Anthony, who was visiting her brother in Kansas. "Woman's cause is in deep water . . . Come back and help. . . . I seem to stand alone."[4]

Anthony returned to New York, and together she and Cady Stanton circulated petitions calling for women's right to vote. They managed to gather only 13,000 signatures. In her autobiography, Cady Stanton reflected:

> *During the six years they . . . labored to inspire the people with enthusiasm for the great measures of the Republican party, [women] were highly honored as 'wise, loyal, and clear-sighted.' But when the*

Lucy Stone argued in favor of voting rights for black men only, despite her active role in the women's suffrage movement.

Lucy Stone, Born Rebel

As a child, Lucy Stone (1818–1893) often heard her father insist that men were superior to women and that women must remain in their proper place. Refusing to accept such restrictions, she was determined to get an education. In 1847, she graduated from Oberlin College, the only college that accepted women at that time. While at Oberlin, Stone was dismayed to find that women were not allowed to join the debating society. Because she wanted to be a public lecturer, she organized a debating society for women, which met in secret. Lucy Stone married Henry Blackwell, a crusader for women's suffrage and, with his approval, kept her maiden name. She lectured throughout the country on abolition and women's rights. In 1869, she established the American Woman Suffrage Association (AWSA), which worked to gain the vote for women through state laws. Beginning in 1870, she and Blackwell published *The Woman's Journal,* one of the longest-running and most influential suffrage papers.

Wendell Phillips believed that gaining voting rights for African-American men was a first priority and that women's suffrage could wait. A staunch abolitionist, Phillips is speaking at an antislavery meeting in Boston in this engraving.

slaves were emancipated, and these women asked that they should be recognized in the reconstruction as citizens of the Republic, equal before the law, all these transcendent virtues vanished like dew before the morning sun.[5]

The Kansas Campaign

In 1866, Cady Stanton and Anthony campaigned for a New York bill that would grant suffrage to women within the state. The bill met with severe opposition. Many men, and a discouraging number of women, claimed that equal rights would upset the balance within the family. Politics was the domain of men, it was argued, and the home was women's sphere. Horace Greeley wrote, "we are satisfied that public sentiment does not demand and would not sustain an innovation so revolutionary and sweeping."[6] The women's suffrage measure was soundly defeated.

Meanwhile, Lucy Stone and her husband, Henry Blackwell, were campaigning for African-American and women's suffrage in Kansas. They urged Cady Stanton and Anthony to join them. For the first time since 1861, Cady Stanton left her family and set out with Anthony on a long lecture tour. To cover as much ground as possible, the women traveled separately in Kansas. The state's former governor, Charles Robinson, accompanied Cady Stanton. They traveled by horse-drawn wagon from one frontier town to the next. "As there were no roads or guideposts, we often lost our way," Cady Stanton recalled. "In going through cañyons and fording streams it was often so dark that the Governor was obliged to walk ahead to find the way, taking off his coat so that I could see his white shirt and slowly drive after him."[7]

Cady Stanton lectured two or three times a day, six days a week, and sometimes once on Sundays as well. She spoke in schoolhouses, churches, courthouses, barns, and open fields. She might have only two dozen people in her audience, but she seized every chance to talk about the need for universal suffrage.

Used to relative luxury, Cady Stanton cheerfully took on the challenges of frontier life. In her letters, she complained about the dirt and the bad food, and longed for soft clean sheets. But she wrote to her husband, "This is the country for us to move to. . . . Ponies are cheap here, so that all our children could ride and breathe, and learn to do big things. I cannot endure the thoughts of living again that contracted eastern existence."[8]

Despite the best efforts of the suffragists, the Kansas bill went down in defeat in November 1867. Yet Cady Stanton and Anthony returned from Kansas with renewed hope. On the campaign trail Cady Stanton had met George Francis Train, an enthusiastic champion of women's rights. Train promised to support them in their efforts. He would finance a women's suffrage newspaper, to be called *The Revolution*.

A Strange Alliance

George Francis Train was immensely wealthy and wildly eccentric. Tall, handsome, and very dramatic, he had ambitions to run for president. In addition to women's suffrage, he supported paper currency, the eight-hour workday, and the cause of independence for Ireland. However, he had been a slaveholder in the south, and he declared unashamedly that African Americans were inferior to whites.

Cady Stanton had worked for the rights of African Americans since she was a teenager visiting her cousin Gerrit Smith in Peterboro. Yet, because he was willing to fight for women's suffrage, she embraced an alliance with the openly racist George Francis Train. Most reformers were appalled. "He may be of use in drawing an audience," warned William Lloyd Garrison, "but so would a kangaroo, a gorilla or a hippopotamus."[9] Lucy

Stone wrote, "Mr. Train is a lunatic, wild and ranting. [His] presence as an advocate of woman suffrage was enough to condemn it in the minds of all persons not already convinced."[10] Cady Stanton did not waver. "It would be right and wise to accept aid from the devil himself," she hurled back, "provided he did not tempt us to lower our standard."[11]

Train's influence strengthened a new set of arguments for women's suffrage that Cady Stanton had begun to form. She claimed that uneducated African-American and immigrant men should not be made politically superior to educated women. To the dismay of her old friends and admirers, her arguments rang with elitism and racism. As momentum grew for a Fifteenth Amendment that would even more clearly guarantee voting rights for African-American males, Cady Stanton said, "Think of Patrick and Sambo and Hans and Yung Tung, . . . who cannot read the Declaration of Independence . . . making laws for . . . the daughters of Adams and Jefferson."[12]

On January 8, 1868, the first edition of *The Revolution* rolled off the presses. The masthead carried the slogan: "Principle, Not Policy; Justice, Not Favors— Men, Their Rights and Nothing More; Women, Their Rights and Nothing Less."[13] *The Revolution* printed articles by Train on Irish independence and other issues he supported. For Cady Stanton, the paper served as a platform for tirades against what she called "an aristocracy of sex." She also returned to her earlier themes of inequality in marriage and the need for fair divorce laws. She compared marriage to a form of slavery and stated in one article that "the 'legal position' of a wife is more dependent and degrading than any other condition of womanhood could possibly be."[14]

Since childhood, Cady Stanton had believed that women were equal to men. At this time, she took a new stance. She argued that women were not merely equal to men, but morally superior. "Woman knows the cost of life better than man does," she wrote in *The Revolution,* "hence her quick sympathy for suffering, her impulse to save and protect life."[15] In another piece she raged, "The male element is a destructive force, stern, selfish, aggrandizing, loving war, violence, conquest, acquisition, breeding in the material and moral world alike discord, disorder, disease, and death."[16]

The sense of betrayal by once-staunch women's suffragists threw Cady Stanton into a state of anger. In a letter to Martha Wright she exclaimed:

> *[It] is enough to rouse one's blood to the white heat of rebellion against every 'white male' on the Continent. When I think of all the wrongs that have been heaped upon womankind, I am ashamed that I am not forever in a condition of chronic wrath, stark mad, skin and bone, my eyes a fountain of tears, my lips overflowing with curses, and my hand raised against every man and brother!*[17]

After *The Revolution*'s first year, Train's interest in the paper began to fade. He traveled to England, and was sent to jail for his anti-British efforts in Ireland. His contributions to *The Revolution* evaporated. After two-and-a-half years of publication, the paper was sold in

The Revolution.

PRINCIPLE, NOT POLICY; JUSTICE, NOT FAVORS.

VOL. I.—NO. 1.   NEW YORK, WEDNESDAY, JANUARY 8, 1868. $2.00 A YEAR.

The Revolution;

THE ORGAN OF THE

NATIONAL PARTY OF NEW AMERICA.

PRINCIPLE, NOT POLICY—INDIVIDUAL RIGHTS AND
RESPONSIBILITIES.

THE REVOLUTION WILL ADVOCATE:

1. IN POLITICS—Educated Suffrage, Irrespective of
Sex or Color; Equal Pay to Women for Equal Work;
Eight Hours Labor; Abolition of Standing Armies and
Party Despotisms. Down with Politicians—Up with the
People!

2. IN RELIGION—Deeper Thought; Broader Idea;
Science not Superstition; Personal Purity; Love to Man
as well as God.

3. IN SOCIAL LIFE—Morality and Reform; Practical
Education, not Theoretical; Facts not Fiction; Virtue not Vice; Cold Water not Alcoholic Drinks or Medi-
cines. It will indulge in no Gross Personalities and in-
sert no Quack or Immoral Advertisements, so common
even in Religious Newspapers.

4. THE REVOLUTION proposes a new Commercial and
Financial Policy. America no longer led by Europe.
Gold like our Cotton and Corn for sale. Greenbacks for
money. An American System of Finance. American
Products and Labor Free. Foreign Manufacturers Pro-
hibited. Open doors to Artisans and Immigrants.
Atlantic and Pacific Oceans for American Steamships
and Shipping; or American goods in American bottoms.
New York the Financial Centre of the World. Wall
Street emancipated from Bank of England, or Ameri-
can Cash for American Bills. The Credit Foncier and
Credit Mobilier System, or Capital Mobilized to Re-
sustitate the South and our Mining Interests, and to
People the Country from Ocean to Ocean, from Omaha
to San Francisco. More organized Labor, more Cotton,
more Gold and Silver Bullion to sell foreigners at the
highest prices. Ten millions of Naturalized Citizens
DEMAND A PENNY OCEAN POSTAGE, to Strengthen the
Brotherhood of Labor; and if Congress Vote One Hundred and Twenty-five Millions for a Standing Army and
Freedmen's Bureau, cannot they spare One Million to
Educate Europe and to keep bright the chain of acquaint-
ance and friendship between those millions and their
fatherlands!

Send in your Subscription. THE REVOLUTION, published weekly, will be the Great Organ of the Age.

TERMS.—Two dollars a year, in advance. Ten names
($20) entitle the sender to one copy free.

ELIZABETH CADY STANTON, } EDS.
PARKER PILLSBURY,

SUSAN B. ANTHONY,
Proprietor and Manager.
37 Park Row (Room 17), New York City,
To whom address all business letters.

KANSAS.

THE question of the enfranchisement of woman has already passed the court of moral discussion, and is now fairly ushered into the arena
of politics, where it must remain a fixed element of debate, until party necessity shall com-
pel its success.

With 9,000 votes in Kansas, one-third the
entire vote, every politician must see that
the friends of "woman's suffrage" hold the
balance of power in that State to-day. And
those 9,000 votes represent a principle deep in
the hearts of the people, for this triumph was
secured without money, without a press, without a party. With these instrumentalities now
fast coming to us on all sides, the victory in
Kansas is but the herald of greater victories in
every State of the Union. Kansas already leads
the world in her legislation for woman on questions of property, education, wages, marriage
and divorce. Her best universities are open
alike to boys and girls. In fact woman has a
voice in the legislation of that State. She votes
on all school questions and is eligible to the
office of trustee. She has a voice in temperance too; no license is granted without the consent of a majority of the adult citizens, male and
female, black and white. The consequence is,
some school houses are voted up in every part
of the State, and rum voted down. Many of
the ablest men in that State are champions
of woman's cause. Governors, judges, lawyers
and clergymen. Two-thirds of the press and
pulpits advocate the idea, in spite of the opposition of politicians. The first Governor of
Kansas, twice chosen to that office, Charles
Robinson, went all through the State, speaking
every day for two months in favor of woman's
suffrage. In the organization of the State
government, he proposed that the words
"white !male" should not be inserted in the
Kansas constitution. All this shows that giving political rights to women is no new idea in
that State. Who that has listened with tearful
eyes to the deep experiences of those Kansas
women, through the darkest hours of their history, does not feel that such bravery and self
denial as they have shown alike in war and
peace, have richly earned for them the crown of
citizenship.

Opposed to this moral sentiment of the lib-
eral minds of the State, many adverse influ-
ences were brought to bear through the entire
campaign.

The action of the New York Constitutional
Convention; the silence of eastern journals on
the question; the opposition of abolitionists
lost a demand for woman's suffrage should defeat negro suffrage; the hostility everywhere of
black men themselves; some even stumping
the State against woman's suffrage; the official
action of both the leading parties in their conventions in Leavenworth against the propo-
sition, with every organized Republican influ-

ence outside as well as inside the State, all combined might have made our vote comparatively
a small one, had not George Francis Train gone
into the State two weeks before the election and
galvanized the Democrats into their duty, thus
securing 9,000 votes for woman's suffrage. Some
claim that we are indebted to the Republicans
for this vote; but the fact that the most radical
republican district, Douglas County, gave the
largest vote against woman's suffrage, while
Leavenworth, the Democratic district, gave the
largest vote for it, fully settles that question.

In saying that Mr. Train helped to swell our
vote takes nothing from the credit due all those
who labored faithfully for months in that State.
All praise to Olympia Brown, Lucy Stone,
Susan B. Anthony, Henry B. Blackwell, and
Judge Wood, who welcomed, for an idea, the
hardships of travelling in a new State, fording
streams, scaling rocky brinks, sleeping on the
ground and eating hard tack, with the fatigue
of constant speaking, in school-houses, barns,
mills, depots and the open air; and especially,
all praise to the glorious Hutchinson family—
John, his son Henry and daughter, Viola—who,
with their own horses and carriage, made the
entire circuit of the state, singing Woman's
Suffrage into souls that logic could never pene-
trate. Having shared with them the hardships,
with them I rejoice in our success.

E. C. S.

THE BALLOT—BREAD, VIRTUE, POWER.

THE REVOLUTION will contain a series of articles, beginning next week, to prove the power
of the ballot in elevating the character and condition of woman. We shall show that the ballot
will secure for woman equal place and equal
wages in the world of work; that it will open
to her the schools, colleges, professions and all
the opportunities and advantages of life; that
in her hand it will be a moral power to stay the
tide of vice and crime and misery on every side.
In the words of Bishop Simpson.—

"We believe that the great vices in our large cities will
never be conquered until the ballot is put in the hands
of women. If the question of the danger of their sons
being drawn away into drinking saloons was brought up,
if the mothers had the power, they would close them;
if the sisters had the power, and they saw their brothers
going away to haunts of infamy, they would close those
places. You may get men to trifle with purity, with
virtue, with righteousness; but, thank God, the hearts
of the women of our land—the mothers, wives and
daughters—are too pure to make a compromise either
with intemperance or licentiousness."

Thus, too, shall we purge our constitutions
and statute laws from all invidious distinctions
among the citizens of the States, and secure
the same civil and moral code for man and
woman. We will show the hundred thousand
female teachers, and the millions of laboring
women, that their complaints, petitions, strikes
and protective unions are of no avail until they
hold the ballot in their own hands; for it is the
first step toward social, religious and political
equality.

This is the first page of the first issue of The Revolution. *The newspaper was not successful and only lasted about a year.*

May 1870. By the time it shut down operations, *The Revolution* had amassed debts of $10,000. Cady Stanton wanted nothing more to do with the enterprise. As an unmarried woman Anthony had signed the contracts for the purchase of paper, printing presses, and other necessities. Cady Stanton refused to help pay the money that was owed. "You know when I drop anything I drop it absolutely," she wrote to Anthony. "You cannot imagine what a deep gulf lies between me and the past."[18] On her own, Susan B. Anthony had to pay off the paper's debts—an effort that took several years.

A Bitter Break

In 1868, Cady Stanton used some of the money she had inherited from her father to buy a house in Tenafly, New Jersey. It was a big, rambling structure with a wide porch, surrounded by gardens. It was only a mile from the train station, and Henry Stanton had an easy commute to his job in New York. As time passed, however, he spent more and more time at the family's apartment in the city, while his wife stayed at the house in Tenafly. For years, the Stantons had lived very separate lives within their marriage. Gradually and peacefully, they slipped into a physical separation as well. They still made decisions together regarding their children, but in most other matters they lived on their own.

In May 1869, Elizabeth Cady Stanton chaired a meeting of the AERA, in the absence of President Lucretia Mott. Her racist comments in *The Revolution* and elsewhere had eroded her support within the AERA.

One delegate, Stephen Foster of Massachusetts, called for her to resign. At the end of a stormy meeting, Cady Stanton invited the group's female members to join her for a reception at *The Revolution*'s office. There, with a small following that included Lucretia Mott and Libby Smith Miller, she formed a new organization, the National Woman Suffrage Association (NWSA).

Supporters of African-American suffrage were hard at work to secure the passage of a Fifteenth Amendment to the Constitution. The proposed amendment stated that the voting rights of U.S. citizens could not be denied on the basis of "race, color, or previous condition of servitude." To Cady Stanton's outrage, gender was not included. The NWSA's mission was to support a Sixteenth Amendment to the Constitution, an amendment that would give the vote to women. It also would uphold the cause of women's rights in education, marriage, and the workplace.

The formation of the NWSA inspired Lucy Stone and her supporters to establish another women's rights organization. The American Woman Suffrage Association (AWSA) did not support a Sixteenth Amendment. Instead, its members pledged to work for the passage of women's suffrage laws state by state.

The founding of the NWSA and AWSA left the women's rights movement divided into separate factions. Although they shared the common cause of women's suffrage, the organizations worked separately and viewed each other with suspicion. The women's rights movement, which began with a sense of energy and unity in 1848, was now bitterly divided.

Chapter 6

Travels and Trials

The break with her old circle of reformers and the division within the women's movement left Elizabeth Cady Stanton feeling drained and discouraged. In 1870, she launched a new strategy to bring about change. Instead of battling for women's suffrage legislation, she determined to educate the women of the nation. When women recognized their oppression and saw their possibilities, she believed, they would begin to fight for their rights.

Taking to the Road

In 1869, Cady Stanton registered as a public lecturer with the Lyceum Bureau of New York. By this time, most of her children were adults living on their own, freeing her to travel. The bureau arranged a speaking tour for her that ran from October through June, with a month off for the Christmas holidays. For eight months of the year she was away from home, lecturing on women's issues from Maine to California. After her first year, she wrote gleefully to Gerrit Smith that she had earned two thousand dollars, "besides stirring up the women generally to rebellion."[1]

For years Cady Stanton had hungered for the freedom to travel and work for women's rights. But she discovered that life on the road had its hardships. When she crossed paths with other Lyceum lecturers, they eagerly commiserated about "the long journeys and the hard fare in the country hotels, . . . the overheated, badly ventilated [railway] cars; the halls, sometimes too warm, sometimes too cold; babies crying in our audiences; the rain pattering on the roof overhead or leaking on the platform."[2] She traveled by train, steamboat, and stagecoach. Once, when a blizzard buried the roads in northern Iowa, she made her way from town to town in a horse-drawn sleigh.

Described as "plump" in the 1860s, Cady Stanton had become seriously overweight. She struggled in and out of stagecoaches, and could seldom make herself comfortable on the hard, narrow beds in small-town hotels. Nevertheless, she made the most of her travels and treated the mild discomforts with her usual good humor.

Nearly everywhere she went, crowds packed the halls to hear Cady Stanton speak. Women pressed around her, pouring out their stories of unhappy marriages and blighted hopes. Admiring young girls asked for her autograph or a lock of her hair.

Not everyone in the audiences agreed with her and applauded. An Illinois woman wrote that she was going to hear "that disgusting old female Cady Stanton." She explained, "I shall go to hear her out of curiosity, she is one of the notorieties in an age full of shams."[3] With her plump, motherly figure, her beautiful white hair and warm, compelling voice, Cady Stanton often won over the doubters. Mrs. Stanton was so delightful, "my pail full of arguments against is getting emptied and the pail of arguments for is filling up," wrote Mary Adams of Iowa.[4] Adams became an active suffragist.

During her years on the lecture circuit, Cady Stanton attended few women's rights conventions, and was relatively inactive in the NWSA. However, her message to women was what it had always been. "As long as man makes, interprets, and executes the laws for himself, he holds the power under any system," she declared in her lecture entitled "Home Life." "Hence when he expresses the fear that liberty for woman would upset the family relation, he acknowledges that her present

> "As long as man makes, interprets, and executes the laws for himself, he holds the power under any system."

condition of subjection is not of her own choosing, and that if she had the power the whole relation would be essentially changed."[5]

A Troubled Friendship

When Cady Stanton skipped the women's rights convention in 1871, Susan B. Anthony was outraged. "To my mind there was never such a suicidal letting go as has been yours these last two years," she wrote to her friend. "How you can excuse yourself is more than I can understand."[6] For Anthony, organizations and conventions were essential to the movement's efforts. While Cady Stanton zigzagged across the country, talking to women about their conditions and their rights, she neglected the organization that was working to promote women's suffrage legislation.

In the early fall of 1871, Cady Stanton and Anthony set out on a lecture tour together. At first it seemed that the trip would heal their differences and strengthen the bond between them. "We have a drawing-room all to ourselves, and here we are just as cozy and happy as lovers," Anthony wrote in the first weeks of the tour.[7] But soon old annoyances flared again. Anthony scolded Cady Stanton for not attending conventions and for not writing enough articles. She nagged her about her habit of snacking. When they went riding together in California's Yosemite, Cady Stanton's horse struggled to carry her weight.

Worst of all, from Anthony's point of view, was the public's response when she and Cady Stanton shared

Elizabeth Cady Stanton and Susan B. Anthony had this photograph taken of them around 1870. Although they went on a lecture tour together in 1871, the two of them had a turbulent friendship during that time.

the speaking platform. Audiences adored Cady Stanton, and she loved connecting with people of all ages and backgrounds. Beside her, Anthony seemed humorless and drab. Sometimes the crowd booed Anthony, while Cady Stanton received wild applause. In her diary Anthony wrote, "Never in all my hard experience have I been under such fire."[8]

Cady Stanton's trip was cut short when she received word that her mother was gravely ill. After her father's death in 1859, she and her mother had grown closer. Margaret Cady had often helped care for the Stanton children while her daughter was traveling. Cady Stanton hurried to Johnstown to be at her mother's bedside. Margaret Stanton died a week after Cady Stanton arrived. In the obituary, Cady Stanton wrote that her mother had hoped to vote before she died.

The New Departure

In 1869, a Missouri suffragist named Virginia Minor and her husband, Francis, conceived a new argument in favor of women's right to vote. The Minors pointed out that the Fourteenth Amendment declares that "all persons born or naturalized in the United States . . . are citizens of the United States." Therefore, as citizens, women already had the right to vote. The argument was so simple and logical that it became known as the New Departure.

In 1872, a suffragist named Victoria Woodhull burst onto the scene, brandishing the New Departure argument in a series of eloquent speeches. Woodhull even delivered a speech on the New Departure before Congress. Since women had the right to vote, she believed, they also had the right to run for office. Woodhull founded the Equal Rights Party so that she could run for president on its ticket.

At first, Cady Stanton was wary of Woodhull, who acted brazenly on her own without consulting established women's rights leaders. When she met Woodhull in person, however, she was dazzled by her beauty and charm. For a time she became one of Woodhull's staunchest supporters. However, Woodhull soon proved

Victoria Woodhull, The First Woman to Run for President

Victoria Claflin Woodhull (1838–1927) loved the spotlight. She began her public career selling patent medicine in carnival tents in Ohio and New York. By 1870, she joined the world of finance as a stockbroker on Wall Street. Woodhull spoke out for a woman's right to end an unhappy marriage through divorce. She became an eloquent suffragist and, in 1872, ran for president on the ticket of the Equal Rights Party. With her sister, Tennessee Claflin, she published a suffragist paper called *Woodhull and Claflin's Weekly* from 1870 to 1876. Victoria Woodhull moved to England in 1876. After a few years as a women's rights activist there, she quietly retired.

Victoria Woodhull delivering her New Departure argument before the Judiciary Committee of the House of Representatives. Elizabeth Cady Stanton is seated behind her in this illustration.

to be an embarrassment to the women's movement, involving Cady Stanton and others in a series of highly publicized scandals. Anthony laid much of the blame at Cady Stanton's feet. In her diary she wrote, "There never was such a foolish muddle—all come of Mrs. S. consulting and conceding to Woodhull. I never was so hurt by the folly of Stanton."[9]

Inspired by the New Departure, Susan B. Anthony and about 150 other U.S. women went to the polls in the presidential election of 1872. The startled election officials allowed them to register and cast their votes. Three weeks later, Anthony was arrested and charged with having voted unlawfully. She hoped that her case would go to the U.S. Supreme Court, and that it would open the way for women to vote legally. However, to her disappointment the case was settled in a lower court in New York. She was fined one hundred dollars, which she never paid. Cady Stanton did not attempt to vote, and remained distant from Anthony's actions. She believed that education, not protest, was the way to bring about change.

In 1875, the U.S. Supreme Court finally heard a case based on the New Departure argument. Unanimously the justices ruled that the term "citizen" merely meant "a member of a nation." It did not confer the right to vote.

Home at Last

During the summers Cady Stanton returned to Tenafly, where she worked on her lectures for the coming season. Henry Stanton left his city apartment and joined her for weeks at a time. He spent most of his time reading in a comfortable chair on the porch. These leisurely summer days gave the couple an occasional chance to reconnect after months apart. All of the children were grown, and Cady Stanton loved watching their first steps into adulthood. She wrote in her autobiography, "Sons and daughters graduating from college, bringing troops of young friends to visit us; . . . weddings, voyages to Europe, business ventures—in this whirl of plans and projects our heads, hearts, and hands were fully occupied."[10]

On her sixty-fifth birthday Elizabeth Cady Stanton began to keep a diary. "Today I am sixty-five years old, am perfectly well, am a moderate eater, sleep well, and am generally happy," she wrote on the first page. She said that it was her life philosophy to "live one day at a time."[11]

Despite Cady Stanton's cheerful outlook, the hardships of the lecture circuit had begun to wear on her. "I have been wandering, wandering," she wrote to Libby Smith Miller in the late 1870s. "Two months more, containing sixty-one days, still stretch their long

Elizabeth Cady Stanton (standing at left) speaking to the Senate Committee in 1878. Throughout the 1870s, Cady Stanton was on the lecture circuit. She retired from the Lyceum Bureau in 1881 after twelve years on the road.

length before me. I must pack and unpack my trunk sixty-one times; . . . shake hands with sixty-one more committees, smile, try to look intelligent and interested in everyone who approaches me, while I feel like a squeezed sponge."[12] In 1881, at the age of sixty-six, she retired from the Lyceum Bureau after her twelfth season on the road. Settled at the house in Tenafly she wrote in her diary, "I do not believe there ever was a woman who esteemed it such a privilege to stay at home."[13]

> "I do not believe there ever was a woman who esteemed it such a privilege to stay at home."

It was not in Cady Stanton's nature to enjoy an idle retirement. As soon as the rigors of the road were behind her, she threw herself into a fresh project—the creation of a detailed history of the women's suffrage movement. Teaming with Susan B. Anthony and suffragist Matilda Joslyn Gage, she gathered and organized thousands of documents related to the suffrage movement. The women wove newspaper accounts, letters, resolutions, and minutes from meetings into a massive work entitled *The History of Woman Suffrage.*

Work on the *History* brought Anthony and Cady Stanton into close contact again. Once more, Anthony moved into her special room at the Tenafly house. As always, she was the main organizer, while Cady Stanton did most of the actual writing. Conflict still flared between the two friends, but through it all they managed to work together. Gage, who was in poor health, took a small part in producing the first volume of the work. Years later, Cady Stanton's older daughter, Margaret Stanton Lawrence, described their typical workday:

> *Everything is harmonious for a season but after straining their eyes over the most illegible, disorderly manuscripts . . . suddenly the whole sky is overspread with dark and threatening clouds. . . . Sometimes these disputes run so high that down go the pens, one sails out one door and one out the other, . . . and just as I have made up my mind that this beautiful friendship of forty years has at last terminated, I see them walking down the hill, arm in arm. . . . They never explain, nor apologize, nor shed tears, nor make up, as other people do.[14]*

The first volume of *The History of Woman Suffrage* was published in 1881. By the time it appeared, Cady Stanton, Anthony, and Gage were at work on the second volume. Stanton's daughter Harriot, an active suffragist, wrote the final chapter, which described the schism in the movement between the NWSA and the AWSA. When volume two was off to the publisher, Cady Stanton set out with Harriot on a long trip to Europe.

Across the Atlantic

Forty-two years before, young Elizabeth Cady Stanton was enchanted by her first ocean voyage, and rode in a pull chair to the top of the mast. Now, at sixty-seven, she found travel difficult and painful. She maneuvered

Elizabeth Cady Stanton with her daughter Harriot Stanton Blatch (right) and her granddaughter Nora in 1890. Cady Stanton and Harriot went on several trips to Europe in the 1880s.

slowly and awkwardly down the narrow gangways. The berth in her cabin had to be widened by a foot to accommodate her size.

When the ship docked in France, Cady Stanton's outlook brightened. She and Harriot went sightseeing and met many interesting people. They enjoyed a long visit with her son Theodore Stanton, who had married a French woman. Cady Stanton delighted in her baby granddaughter, named Elizabeth Cady Stanton and nicknamed Lizette.

After several months in France, Cady Stanton and Harriot went to London. Cady Stanton met the leading British suffragists as well as labor reformers and

> **"When the news comes, the heart and pulses all seem to stand still . . ."**

activists in other fields. She also visited Parliament and observed that the suffrage movement in England seemed to face the same obstacles that made its progress so slow in the United States.

In all her years as a homemaker and activist, Cady Stanton had never before had such an opportunity to relax and enjoy herself. In her diary she wrote, "This is the first time in my life that I have had uninterrupted leisure for reading, free from all care of home, servants, and children."[15] She made several more trips to Europe during the 1880s, altogether spending nearly five years overseas.

Cady Stanton was in England in January of 1887 when a cablegram informed her that Henry Stanton had died of pneumonia. "When the news comes, the heart and pulses all seem to stand still," she wrote in her diary. "Ah! If we could only remember in life to be gentle and forbearing with each other, and to strive to serve nobly instead of exacting service, our memories of the past would be more pleasant."[16] Whatever her regrets may have been, she did not rush back to attend her husband's funeral. In fact, she did not return to the United States for several more months.

Healing the Break

In 1888, to mark the fortieth anniversary of the Seneca Falls Convention, delegates from women's rights organizations in the United States and Europe gathered for a weeklong conference in Washington, D.C. Members of both the AWSA and the NWSA took part. Susan B. Anthony felt that the split had harmed the cause of women's suffrage, and wanted to see the two suffrage associations reunited. She also wanted to merge with the Women's Christian Temperance Union (WCTU). With 150,000 members, the WCTU was the largest and strongest women's organization in the nation. Its members wanted suffrage in order to vote for a federal ban on the sale of alcoholic beverages.

Cady Stanton was wary of the WCTU, with its emphasis on the Christian religion. As time passed, however, she became receptive to the idea of a merger with the AWSA. She realized that many of the younger women who had joined the movement did not care about long-ago differences. They wanted a strong, unified organization that could fight for the cause of suffrage.

By the 1880s, a few of the western territories in the United States had granted suffrage to women. In 1890, Wyoming was admitted into the Union as the first state that permitted women to vote. It was a victory, but only a small one, and Cady Stanton did not rejoice. She felt that the AWSA's efforts to win suffrage state by state had proved a dismal failure. The NWSA's efforts to gain national suffrage had also been unsuccessful. Working separately, the two organizations had made relatively few gains. Perhaps, if they combined their efforts, women's suffrage could be achieved at last.

WOMAN SUFFRAGE IN WYOMING TERRITORY.—SCENE AT THE POLLS IN CHEYENNE.
FROM A PHOTO. BY KIRKLAND.—SEE PAGE 253.

Women voting in the Wyoming Territory on November 24, 1888, in this illustration from Frank Leslie's Illustrated Newspaper. *Wyoming, after becoming a state in 1890, was the first state that permitted women to vote.*

In 1890, the National Woman Suffrage Association and the American Woman Suffrage Association became one, known as the National American Woman Suffrage Association (NAWSA). Anthony and Cady Stanton were both nominated for president. Although Anthony agreed to run for the office, she gave a speech in support of her longtime friend. "I hope you will not vote for [me] for President," she concluded. "Don't vote for any human being but Mrs. Stanton."[17] Lucy Stone and some of her devoted supporters had never forgotten Cady Stanton's elitist comments of the late 1860s or her involvement with George Francis Train. They argued that she should not preside over the new organization. Despite their objections, Elizabeth Cady Stanton was elected to serve as the NAWSA's first president.

Cady Stanton's position as NAWSA president was mainly symbolic. Shortly after her inauguration, she left on another trip to Europe. But her election showed that women in the suffrage movement respected her and honored her unique contributions. As they pushed the movement forward, they wanted her to be with them.

The Solitude of Self

I n 1891, Elizabeth Cady Stanton said her last farewell to England and steamed homeward across the Atlantic. She had received the shocking news that her beloved son Neil had died unexpectedly. After years of travel, she longed to have her family and friends around her.

The Stantons had sold the Tenafly house several years before, and Cady Stanton no longer had a home. Susan B. Anthony invited her to live with her in Rochester.

The Grand Old Woman of America

Despite their many differences and tensions over the years, Cady Stanton and Anthony still held one another dear. "We have jogged along pretty well for forty years or more," Cady Stanton wrote to her friend. "Perhaps mid the wreck of thrones and the undoing of so many friendships, sects, parties and families, you and I deserve some credit for sticking together through all adverse winds with so few ripples on the surface."[1] Nevertheless, she turned down Anthony's offer, explaining that she preferred to live with her children.

With her son Robert and widowed daughter Margaret, Cady Stanton settled into a comfortable Manhattan apartment. The convenience of apartment living delighted her. In her autobiography she wrote, "To be transported from the street to your apartment in an elevator in half a minute, to have all your food and fuel sent to your kitchen by an elevator in the rear, to have your rooms all warmed with no effort of your own, seemed like a realization of some fairy dream."[2]

Elevators were a blessing to Cady Stanton because her weight had become a severe problem. In a letter to a friend she confided that she tipped the scales at 240 pounds.[3] "I cannot clamber up and down platforms, mount long staircases into halls and hotels, be squeezed in the crush at receptions, and do all the other things public life involves," she admitted in her diary.[4] She suffered shortness of breath, and a heart ailment for which doctors could find no cure. Susan B. Anthony lamented, "It is too cruel that such mental powers may be hampered by such a clumsy body."[5]

Cady Stanton's public appearances were few now, but she carried herself regally. She usually wore black silk, and covered her snowy white curls with a lace shawl. Newspaper reporters called her the "Grand Old Woman of America." Yet her message had not lost its bite. Grace Greenwood, a Philadelphia journalist, commented, "Stately Mrs. Stanton has secured much immunity by a comfortable look of motherliness and a sly benignancy in her smiling eyes, even though her arguments have been bayonet thrusts and her words gun shots."[6]

The Final Address

For years, Cady Stanton had summoned little enthusiasm for women's rights organizations. She was skeptical about the work of the NAWSA, and served as president in name only. The decision to close the NAWSA's Washington office dismayed her. She felt that the organization needed to maintain a strong presence in the nation's capital, and closing the national office suggested a weakened resolve to work for a federal women's suffrage law. She believed that NAWSA members were timid, indecisive, and afraid of confrontation. As she stepped down from the presidency in 1892, Cady Stanton declared at the NAWSA convention: "At present our association has so narrowed its platform for reasons of policy and propriety that our conventions have ceased to point the way."[7]

In the final years of her life, newspaper reporters called Elizabeth Cady Stanton the "Grand Old Woman of America." This is a portrait of Cady Stanton in her later years.

The NAWSA convention speech in 1892 was Cady Stanton's last major address. Only two days later, she delivered the same speech before the Senate Committee on Woman Suffrage. Titled "The Solitude of Self," it is regarded as the most masterful speech of her long career.

In "The Solitude of Self," Cady Stanton expressed the philosophy that powered her lifelong commitment to women's rights. She spoke of women's need for self-sovereignty, the capacity to think and act for themselves. She argued that women are taught to rely on others for support and protection, and too often fail to develop their own abilities. Yet all human beings are ultimately alone, and must live as individuals, making choices and acting on their own behalf. She stated in her speech:

> *The strongest reason for giving woman all the opportunities for higher education, for the full development of her faculties, her forces of mind and body; . . . is the solitude and personal responsibility of her own individual life. The strongest reason why we ask for woman a voice in the government under which she lives; in the religion she is asked to believe; equality in social life, where she is the chief factor; a place in the trades and professions, where she may earn her bread, is because of her birthright to self-sovereignty; because, as an individual, she must rely on herself.*[8]

"The Solitude of Self" was reprinted in newspapers across the country. Activists in the women's rights movement gave it high praise. Susan B. Anthony declared that the speech was "the strongest and most unanswerable argument and appeal made by the moral pen or tongue for the full freedom and franchise of women."[9]

Looking Back at Eighty

In honor of Elizabeth Cady Stanton's eightieth birthday on November 12, 1895, her son Theodore Stanton and Susan B. Anthony organized a gala celebration. To accommodate the hundreds of guests, the event was held at New York's Metropolitan Opera House. Gifts, flowers, and telegrams poured in from all over the country, and from friends in Europe. In a glowing tribute, one newspaper editor stated:

> *Every woman who seeks the legal custody of her children; who finds the door of a college or university open to her; who administers a post-office or a public library; who enters upon a career of medicine, law or theology; who teaches school or tills a farm or keeps a shop or rides a bicycle—every such woman owes her liberty largely to yourself and to your earliest and bravest co-workers.*[10]

Cady Stanton was deeply moved by the honors that were heaped upon her. "My birthday celebration, with all the testimonials of love and friendship I received, was an occasion of such serious thought and deep feeling as I had never before experienced," she wrote later.[11] After nearly fifty years of effort, most women in the United States still could not vote. However, the movement that Cady Stanton launched in 1848 had

Higher Education for Women

In 1833, Oberlin College in Ohio became the first U.S. college to admit both women and men. However, the vast majority of colleges and universities were open to men only. In 1837, Mount Holyoke College in South Hadley, Massachusetts, became the nation's first college for women only. Other women's colleges followed: Elmira College in Elmira, New York (1855), Vassar College in Poughkeepsie, New York (1861), and Smith College in Northampton, Massachusetts (1875). Stanford University in Palo Alto, California, was among the first coeducational universities in the United States when it was established in 1885.

Oberlin College was the first U.S. college to admit both men and women. This is a view of the college on June 6, 1891.

overturned centuries of injustice for women. Women were now free to attend many of the nation's colleges and universities. Increasing numbers of women had entered medicine, law, the ministry, and other professions. Many of the cruel laws that Cady Stanton had found in her father's law books had been repealed. Women could own and inherit property, divorce abusive husbands, and gain custody of their children. Furthermore, women had won the right to vote in four states. They could vote in local elections and run for office in many towns and cities across the country.

On the day after her birthday celebration, Cady Stanton sat at the piano in her New York apartment. Later, her nephew Robert Stanton described how she played and sang the

> *old, old songs of her youth, in a voice and manner so beautiful [and] so sad . . . that I was spell bound. Not a word was spoken. She seemed to be far away from us and the throngs that greeted her with so much enthusiasm the night before, and was living over again the days of her youth, seeing life as it was to her sixty or seventy years ago. She finally stopped singing, . . . [she] said, 'Bob, life is a great mystery.' That was all.*[12]

The Woman's Bible

Two weeks after her eightieth birthday, Elizabeth Cady Stanton published the first volume of *The Woman's Bible*. For decades she had been convinced that male priests and ministers twisted scripture to support the position that women were inferior. In 1892, she enlisted the help of several women's rights advocates to search out and comment upon every Biblical reference to women. *The Woman's Bible* was the result of this painstaking work. Each relevant passage was printed in full, followed by commentary that presented a fresh, female-friendly interpretation.

The first section of *The Woman's Bible* began with the familiar story of Adam and Eve in the Garden of Eden. According to the well-known story, God made Adam in his own image, and later created Eve from Adam's rib. *The Woman's Bible* printed that story and another, less familiar chapter of the Book of Genesis states that God made woman and man in his image, both at the same time. According to this Biblical version, woman and man are equally formed in the image of God.

The Woman's Bible sparked a storm of outrage. Ministers railed against it from the pulpit. Newspaper editorials denounced Cady Stanton for unraveling the moral fabric of the Christian world. All the fuss made the public very curious about the book, and people rushed out to buy it. *The Woman's Bible* had seven printings in its first year.

Cady Stanton was delighted by the controversy. With glee she noted that the book made the clergy "jump round . . . like parched peas on a hot shovel."[13] Leaders of the NAWSA, however, were horrified by the book. They feared it would turn the public against their cause of women's suffrage. At the 1895 NAWSA convention, suffragist Carrie Chapman Catt proposed a

Composing *The Woman's Bible*

In 1892, Elizabeth Cady Stanton contacted thirty female scholars, inviting them to write commentaries on Biblical passages about women. Afraid that the project would be too controversial, many scholars refused. Undaunted, Cady Stanton moved ahead with the help of Clara Colby, a women's rights advocate. She bought dozens of inexpensive Bibles and cut out the pages that contained references to women. She pasted these pages into a notebook and wrote her commentaries on the opposite page. She found many instances where women were referred to as cursed, unclean, and subservient to men. However, she also found examples of women who were wise and well respected. Cady Stanton was convinced that women's inferior status was not God's will, but the will of men who had misused the Bible for hundreds of years.

resolution calling on NAWSA to censure Cady Stanton for writing *The Woman's Bible*.

Susan B. Anthony had not taken part in *The Woman's Bible* project, and did not share Cady Stanton's passionate feeling against religious dogma. But she cherished the right of freedom of expression. As the NAWSA debated Catt's resolution, Anthony made an eloquent plea. "You would better not begin resolving against individual action or you will find no limit," she warned. "This year it is Mrs. Stanton; next year it may be I or one of yourselves who may be the victim."[14] Despite Anthony's strong arguments, Catt's resolution was approved.

Cady Stanton published a different book in 1898. Her autobiography, *Eighty Years and More*, chronicled her long life in the women's movement. It described her adventures with gentle humor, and was filled with warm stories about family and friends. The book helped to restore Cady Stanton's motherly image. "An earnest reformer was she, but the volume shows the delight she felt in being an excellent housekeeper and, how, as the mother of a large family, she cared for her children," wrote a reviewer in *The New York Times*. "Mrs. Cady Stanton has shown that some women can advance the social conditions of their own sex and yet be good wives and mothers."[15]

Passing on the Reins

By 1900, Elizabeth Cady Stanton seldom left the apartment she shared with her son Robert. Her failing heart and aching joints, compounded by her massive weight, made even the shortest walks difficult. Her eyesight was

The Woman's Bible

Chapter. II.

by

Elizabeth Cady Stanton

(in small print)

Genesis II 21—25.

21 And the LORD God caused a deep sleep to fall upon Adam, and he slept; and he took one of his ribs, and closed up the flesh instead thereof.
22 And the rib, which the LORD God had taken from man, made he a woman, and brought her unto the man.
23 And Adam said, This is now bone of my bones, and flesh of my flesh: she shall be called Woman, because she was taken out of man.
24 Therefore shall a man leave his father and his mother, and shall cleave unto his wife: and they shall be one flesh.
25 And they were both naked, the man and his wife, and were not ashamed.

As the account of the creation in the first chapter, is in harmony with science, common sense & the experience of mankind in natural laws, the enquiry naturally arises why should there be two contradictory accounts in the same book, of the same event? It is fair to infer that the second version, which is found in some form, in the different religions of all nations, is a mere allegory, symbolizing some mysterious conception of a

This is a draft manuscript page from chapter two of The Woman's Bible. This comes from the collection of Elizabeth Cady Stanton Papers at the Library of Congress. The Woman's Bible caused great public outrage.

failing, and reading tired her. Her devoted children and grandchildren read her the newspapers and the letters from friends that filled her mailbox every day.

For the most part, Cady Stanton accepted the slower pace of life. She realized that she would never see nationwide women's suffrage in her lifetime, but she knew that her work was done. She had launched and sustained a movement that someday would bring justice and freedom to women everywhere.

Susan B. Anthony, too, suffered from failing health. By her eightieth birthday, she was at home with her sister in Rochester, recovering from a stroke. As a birthday greeting, Cady Stanton sent her a long poem that recounted the story of their friendship and their work together. She concluded:

> *To younger hands resign the reins,*
> *With all the honors, and the gains.*[16]

During the spring of 1902, Susan B. Anthony made the journey to New York City for a visit with her old friend. When they said good-bye, she promised to return again in the fall. Cady Stanton spent the summer entertaining visitors and working on articles. Early in October, a New York newspaper published her latest piece on the need for further reform in divorce laws.

Though her mind was as sharp as ever, Cady Stanton's body was failing. When the doctor visited her on the afternoon of Saturday, October 25, she told him, "Now, if you can't cure this difficulty of breathing, and if I am not to feel brighter and more like work again, I want you to give me something to send me pack-horse speed to heaven."[17] Even as death approached, she still wanted to be in control.

The next morning, all six of Cady Stanton's surviving children gathered at her bedside. With help, she rose from her chair and stood for several minutes, her hands resting on the table before her. She gazed ahead, as if she were deep in thought. Her daughter Harriot believed that in her mind she was giving one last address to a rapt audience. At last, she sank onto her chair again and fell asleep. Elizabeth Cady Stanton died on October 26, 1902, less than three weeks before her eighty-seventh birthday. According to her wishes, Cady Stanton was honored with a simple memorial service at her apartment. She was then buried in New York's Woodlawn Cemetery.

Elizabeth Cady Stanton had touched millions of lives. Her family received a flood of letters from friends and total strangers, offering their heartfelt condolences. Newspapers across the country printed obituaries that praised Cady Stanton's life of dedication.

One of the most moving tributes to Cady Stanton was written by her friend and fellow suffragist Helen Gardener. "In her the world has lost its greatest woman, its noblest mother, its clearest thinker," Gardener wrote. "She embraced in her motherhood all who were under the ban of oppression; she thought for the thoughtless of whatever sex; she was great enough to be honest with her own soul, and to walk in the light of the sun, hand in hand with the naked Truth! And in this she stood almost alone."[18]

A Legacy of Equality

O n February 15, 1906, Susan B. Anthony traveled to Washington, D.C., for a gala eighty-sixth birthday celebration. Cards and telegrams poured in from well-wishers. Even President Theodore Roosevelt sent his fond regards. Anthony was frail and ill, but she managed to give an inspiring speech to her friends and admirers. She urged them to continue in the struggle for women's suffrage. At the close she stated, "Failure is impossible."[1] About three weeks later, Susan B. Anthony died at her home in Rochester.

A New Generation

Elizabeth Cady Stanton and Susan B. Anthony, two of the most powerful forces behind the women's rights movement, were gone. Yet, as Cady Stanton had foreseen, a new generation of leaders took the reins. Women such as Harriot Stanton Blatch, Lucy Burns, and Alice Paul experimented with new tactics to propel the movement forward.

In 1912, Theodore Roosevelt ran for another term as president. In his platform, he promised to give women the right to vote. Filled with new hope, suffragists threw themselves into the Roosevelt campaign.

After the death of Cady Stanton and Anthony, a new generation of leaders took over the women's rights movement. Harriot Stanton Blatch speaks to a crowd on Wall Street in New York City.

To their bitter disappointment, Roosevelt lost to the anti-suffrage candidate, Woodrow Wilson.

On March 3, 1913, the day before Wilson's inauguration, some seven thousand women and men gathered in Washington for a spectacular women's suffrage march. The parade included twenty-six floats, ten bands, and six golden chariots. Leading the march were women from New Zealand, Australia, Finland, and Norway—nations that had already granted voting rights to women.

Crowds of spectators jammed the streets. Many were supportive, but some hurled insults. Heckling turned to violence as spectators grabbed marchers and pulled them to the ground. More than one hundred people had to be taken to the hospital. One newspaper reported, "[Ambulances] came and went constantly for six hours, always impeded and at times actually opposed" by the crowd.[2]

The violence at the parade shocked the public. Some people who had opposed women's suffrage became more sympathetic to the cause. Over the next few years, even Woodrow Wilson changed his mind and declared that women should be enfranchised, by an amendment to the United States Constitution.

Winning the Right to Vote

Around the world, women's suffrage was gaining momentum. By 1918, women in Austria, Canada, Czechoslovakia, Germany, Hungary, Ireland, and Poland were going to the polls. For the first time, the U.S. House of Representatives passed a resolution favoring a

A view of the women's suffrage parade in Washington, D.C., on March 3, 1913. The violence that occurred during the parade brought more support to the women's suffrage cause.

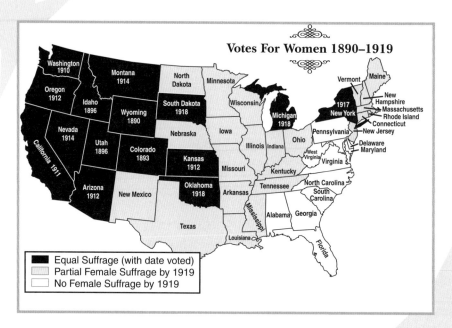

Votes For Women 1890–1919

Legend:
- ■ Equal Suffrage (with date voted)
- ▦ Partial Female Suffrage by 1919
- □ No Female Suffrage by 1919

This map shows the states that allowed women to vote before the Nineteenth Amendment to the Constitution was ratified.

women's suffrage amendment to the Constitution. However, a new wave of antisuffrage feeling swelled across the country. Men and women hoisted up all the old arguments—a woman's proper place was the home; a woman's mind could not grasp political issues; an interest in politics would destroy a woman's femininity. The Senate voted down the resolution.

Undaunted, the suffragists pressed on. In 1919, another suffrage resolution moved through Congress. This time it passed in both the House and the Senate. Suffragists were exultant. "We can turn our backs upon the end of a long and arduous struggle," said Carrie Chapman Catt, "needlessly darkened and embittered by the stubbornness of a few at the expense of the many."[3]

The battle was not yet over. In order to become a constitutional amendment, the resolution required the approval of three-fourths of the forty-seven states which then comprised the nation. State by state, the suffragists worked to win the amendment's passage. In July 1920, Tennessee became the thirty-sixth state to ratify the amendment, completing the three-fourths approval that was needed.

The Nineteenth Amendment to the Constitution, sometimes known as the Anthony Amendment, was officially adopted on August 26, 1920. Seventy-two years had passed since Elizabeth Cady Stanton called together the first women's rights convention in Seneca Falls. She had sparked a rebellion that had not been quenched by insult or setback. At last, in the presidential election of 1920, women flocked to the polls to exercise their hard-won right to vote as full citizens of their country.

The Struggle for Equal Rights

To Elizabeth Cady Stanton, gaining the right to vote was only one of the hurdles women had to overcome. Through her writings and speeches, she spoke out about women's unequal status in marriage, education, and the workforce. She even challenged religious beliefs that upheld the notion of women's inferiority to men. She never claimed that suffrage alone would lift women to true equality.

In 1923, at the seventy-fifth anniversary celebration of the Seneca Falls Convention, Alice Paul proposed another constitutional amendment. The Equal Rights

Amendment, as it came to be known, would insure full equality of the sexes under the law. The Equal Rights Amendment (ERA) was introduced to Congress later that year, but failed to pass.

Like the Anthony Amendment, the ERA was introduced to Congress year after year for decades. At last, in 1972, both the Senate and the House of Representatives approved the amendment. Congress allowed seven years for it to be ratified by three-fourths of the states—thirty-eight of the fifty states. Despite their many years of effort, women's rights activists were unable to secure enough state ratifications to turn the measure into law.

At the beginning of the twenty-first century, women in the United States still did not enjoy complete equality with men. Men still far outnumbered women in politics and in the upper realms of the corporate world. Women's earnings remained much lower than those of male workers. Women still bore the heaviest responsibility for raising and supporting children. Women in the workforce often received inadequate family leave when they gave birth or adopted a child.

Nevertheless, although the United States has no Equal Rights Amendment, equality of the sexes has become more and more widely accepted. Today, women are admitted to nearly all of the colleges and universities that once were open only to men. Women work in virtually every occupation, and are active in all branches of the armed services. Equal pay for equal work has become standard practice.

In the United States today, it is hard to imagine a world in which women could not inherit property or

Representative Carolyn Maloney of New York speaks at a news conference to reintroduce the Equal Rights Amendment (ERA) to the Constitution on March 15, 2005, in Washington, D.C. Since Alice Paul first proposed the amendment in 1923, women's rights activists have been trying to get it passed.

keep their earnings. It is hard to remember that only a few generations ago, fathers had absolute control over their children's fate. The idea that husband and wife are one, and that that "one" is the husband, seems little more than a historical oddity.

Elizabeth Cady Stanton helped to found one of the world's great movements. The Seneca Falls Convention triggered a revolution that transformed life in the United States. The girl who rebelled against cruel laws spent her life in an unrelenting struggle to bring about social justice.

1815—**November 12:** Elizabeth Cady is born in Johnstown, New York.

1830—After graduating from the Johnstown Academy, Elizabeth Cady enters Miss Willard's Seminary for Girls in Troy, New York.

1840—Marries abolitionist Henry B. Stanton and attends the International Antislavery Convention in London, where she meets women's rights advocate Lucretia Mott.

1848—Organizes the world's first women's rights convention in Seneca Falls, New York; she declares that women should have the right to vote.

1851—Cady Stanton meets Susan B. Anthony, who becomes her close friend and partner in the fight for women's suffrage.

1852—Susan B. Anthony forms the Women's New York State Temperance Society, and Elizabeth Cady Stanton is elected as president of the group.

1854—Cady Stanton delivers an address on women's rights to the New York State Legislature in Albany.

1861—Anthony and Cady Stanton give a series of antislavery lectures in New York State.

1862—Henry Stanton is put in charge of the customs house in New York City, and the Stanton family leaves Seneca Falls.

1863—Cady Stanton founds the National Woman's Loyal League to press for an end to slavery in the United States.

1866—Cady Stanton and Anthony are elected to the executive board of the American Equal Rights Association, committed to promoting equality for African Americans and women.

1867—With Susan B. Anthony and Lucy Stone, Cady Stanton campaigns in Kansas for voting rights for women and African Americans.

1868—Cady Stanton and Anthony begin to publish a women's suffrage newspaper called *The Revolution.*

1869—Cady Stanton and Anthony form the National Woman Suffrage Association (NWSA); Lucy Stone and her supporters form a rival organization, the American Woman Suffrage Association (AWSA).

1870—Cady Stanton begins a twelve-year career as a paid lecturer with the Lyceum Bureau of New York.

1881—The first volume of *The History of Woman Suffrage* is published, edited by Elizabeth Cady Stanton, Susan B. Anthony, and Matilda Joslyn Gage.

1882—Cady Stanton leaves for Europe with her daughter Harriot.

1887—Henry Stanton dies.

1890—The NWSA and AWSA merge to form the National American Woman Suffrage Association (NAWSA) with Elizabeth Cady Stanton as president.

1891—Cady Stanton returns from her last visit to Europe and settles in New York City.

1892—Resigning as NAWSA president, Cady Stanton delivers her most famous address, "The Solitude of Self."

1895—The first volume of the controversial book *The Woman's Bible* is published.

1898—Cady Stanton's autobiography, *Eighty Years and More,* is published.

1902—**October 26:** Cady Stanton dies in New York City.

1920—**August 26:** Congress adopts the Nineteenth Amendment to the Constitution, giving women the right to vote in the United States.

CHAPTER NOTES

CHAPTER 1
A Revolution at Seneca Falls

1. Judith Wellman, *The Road to Seneca Falls: Elizabeth Cady Stanton and the First Woman's Rights Convention* (Champaign, Ill.: University of Illinois Press, 2004), p. 189.
2. Ibid., p. 194.
3. Elizabeth Cady Stanton, *Eighty Years and More: 1815–1897; Reminiscences of Elizabeth Cady Stanton* (New York: Source Book Press, 1970), pp. 147–148.
4. Wellman, p. 189.
5. Jeffrey C. Ward, *Not for Ourselves Alone: The Story of Elizabeth Cady Stanton and Susan B. Anthony; An Illustrated History* (New York: Alfred A. Knopf, 1999), p. 58.
6. Wellman, p. 195.
7. Ward, p. 61.
8. Wellman, p. 198.
9. Ibid., p. 208.

CHAPTER 2
"You Should Have Been a Boy"

1. Elizabeth Cady Stanton, *Eighty Years and More: 1815–1897; Reminiscences of Elizabeth Cady Stanton* (New York: Source Book Press, 1970), p. 4.
2. Elisabeth Griffith, *In Her Own Right: The Life of Elizabeth Cady Stanton* (New York: Oxford University Press, 1984), p. 3.
3. Stanton, pp. 10–11.
4. Ibid., p. 5.
5. Ibid., p. 17.
6. Laurel Thatcher Ulrich, *Well-Behaved Women Seldom Make History* (New York: Alfred A. Knopf, 2007), p. 140.

7. Stanton, p. 32.
8. Ibid., pp. 20–21.
9. Ibid., p. 23.
10. Griffith, p. 17.
11. Stanton, p. 41.
12. Alma Lutz, *Created Equal: A Biography of Elizabeth Cady Stanton* (New York: John Day Company, 1940), p. 15.
13. Ibid., p. 21.

CHAPTER 3
Forging a Movement

1. Elizabeth Cady Stanton, *Eighty Years and More: 1815–1897; Reminiscences of Elizabeth Cady Stanton* (New York: Source Book Press, 1970), p. 74.
2. Ibid., p. 80.
3. Ibid., p. 81.
4. Elisabeth Griffith, *In Her Own Right: The Life of Elizabeth Cady Stanton* (New York: Oxford University Press, 1984), p. 36.
5. Ibid., p. 41.
6. Stanton, pp. 120–121.
7. Griffith, p. 42.
8. Stanton, p. 137.
9. Ibid., p. 144.
10. Ibid., p. 145.
11. Judith Wellman, *The Road to Seneca Falls: Elizabeth Cady Stanton and the First Woman's Rights Convention* (Champaign, Ill.: University of Illinois Press, 2004), p. 78.
12. Ibid., p. 128.
13. Ibid., pp. 118–119.

CHAPTER 4
"A Caged Lioness"

1. Elisabeth Griffith, *In Her Own Right: The Life of Elizabeth Cady Stanton* (New York: Oxford University Press, 1984), p. 58.
2. Martha L. Solomon, ed., *A Book of Their Own: The Woman Suffrage Press, 1840–1910* (Tuscaloosa, Ala.: University of Alabama Press, 1993), p. 13.

3. Griffith, p. 58.
4. Ibid.
5. Elizabeth Cady Stanton, *Eighty Years and More: 1815–1897; Reminiscences of Elizabeth Cady Stanton* (New York: Source Book Press, 1970), p. 201.
6. Griffith, p. 68.
7. Ibid., p. 70.
8. Stanton, p. 163.
9. Jeffrey C. Ward, *Not for Ourselves Alone: The Story of Elizabeth Cady Stanton and Susan B. Anthony; An Illustrated History* (New York: Alfred A. Knopf, 1999), p. 67.
10. Ibid., p. 73.
11. Griffith, p. 74.
12. Ibid.
13. Alma Lutz, *Created Equal: A Biography of Elizabeth Cady Stanton* (New York: John Day Company, 1940), p. 100.
14. Stanton, p. 187.
15. Ibid., p. 188.
16. Ward, p. 75.
17. Ellen Carol DuBois, *The Elizabeth Cady Stanton-Susan B. Anthony Reader, Correspondence, Writings, Speeches* (Boston: Northeastern University Press, 1992), p. 63.
18. Ibid., p. 59.
19. Ward, p. 89.
20. Griffith, p. 93.
21. Ibid., p. 90.
22. Dubois, p. 79.

CHAPTER 5
A Divided Sisterhood

1. Jeffrey C. Ward, *Not for Ourselves Alone: The Story of Elizabeth Cady Stanton and Susan B. Anthony; An Illustrated History* (New York: Alfred A. Knopf, 1999), p. 98.
2. Elisabeth Griffith, *In Her Own Right: The Life of Elizabeth Cady Stanton* (New York: Oxford University Press, 1984), p. 112.
3. Ward, p. 103.
4. Ibid.

5. Elizabeth Cady Stanton, *Eighty Years and More: 1815–1897; Reminiscences of Elizabeth Cady Stanton* (New York: Source Book Press, 1970), pp. 240–241.
6. Ward, p. 106.
7. Stanton, p. 247.
8. Griffith, p. 120.
9. Ibid., p. 130.
10. Ibid.
11. Ibid., p. 131.
12. Ward, p. 117.
13. Martha L. Solomon, ed., *A Book of Their Own: The Woman Suffrage Press, 1840–1910* (Tuscaloosa, Ala.: University of Alabama Press, 1993), p. 71.
14. Ibid., p. 77.
15. Ibid., p. 75.
16. Ward, p. 112.
17. Ellen Carol DuBois, *The Elizabeth Cady Stanton-Susan B. Anthony Reader, Correspondence, Writings, Speeches* (Boston: Northeastern University Press, 1992), p. 102.
18. Ward, p. 133.

CHAPTER 6
Travels and Trials

1. Jeffrey C. Ward, *Not for Ourselves Alone: The Story of Elizabeth Cady Stanton and Susan B. Anthony; An Illustrated History* (New York: Alfred A. Knopf, 1999), p. 135.
2. Elizabeth Cady Stanton, *Eighty Years and More: 1815–1897; Reminiscences of Elizabeth Cady Stanton* (New York: Source Book Press, 1970), p. 260.
3. Ward, p. 165.
4. Ibid., p. 169.
5. Ellen Carol DuBois, *The Elizabeth Cady Stanton-Susan B. Anthony Reader, Correspondence, Writings, Speeches* (Boston: Northeastern University Press, 1992), p. 132.
6. Ward, p. 134.
7. Elisabeth Griffith, *In Her Own Right: The Life of Elizabeth Cady Stanton* (New York: Oxford University Press, 1984), p. 150.

8. Ibid., p. 151.
9. Ibid., p. 152.
10. Stanton, p. 322.
11. Griffith, p. 171.
12. Ward, p. 161.
13. Ibid.
14. Ibid., p. 154.
15. Ibid., p. 162.
16. Griffith, p. 188.
17. Ibid., p. 199.

CHAPTER 7
The Solitude of Self

1. Elisabeth Griffith, *In Her Own Right: The Life of Elizabeth Cady Stanton* (New York: Oxford University Press, 1984), p. 182.
2. Elizabeth Cady Stanton, *Eighty Years and More: 1815–1897; Reminiscences of Elizabeth Cady Stanton* (New York: Source Book Press, 1970), p. 432.
3. Jeffrey C. Ward, *Not for Ourselves Alone: The Story of Elizabeth Cady Stanton and Susan B. Anthony; An Illustrated History* (New York: Alfred A. Knopf, 1999), p. 183.
4. Griffith, p. 206.
5. Ibid.
6. Ibid., p. 196.
7. Beth M. Waggenspack, *The Search for Self-Sovereignty: The Oratory of Elizabeth Cady Stanton* (New York: Greenwood Press, 1989), p. 35.
8. Ellen Carol DuBois, *The Elizabeth Cady Stanton-Susan B. Anthony Reader, Correspondence, Writings, Speeches* (Boston: Northeastern University Press, 1992), p. 247.
9. Waggenspack, p. 82.
10. Griffith, p. 209.
11. Stanton, p. 465.
12. Griffith, pp. 209–210.
13. Ibid., p. 212.
14. Ibid., p. 213.

15. Martha Watson, *Lives of Their Own: Rhetorical Dimensions in the Autobiographies of Women Activists* (Columbia, S.C.: University of South Carolina Press, 1999), p. 75.
16. Dubois, p. 294.
17. Ibid., p. 265.
18. Ibid.

CHAPTER 8
A Legacy of Equality

1. Ellen Carol DuBois, *The Elizabeth Cady Stanton-Susan B. Anthony Reader, Correspondence, Writings, Speeches* (Boston: Northeastern University Press, 1992), p. 258.
2. Gina de Angelis, *It Happened in Washington, D.C.* (Guilford, Conn.: Globe Pequot Press, 2004), p. 107.
3. *The New York Times,* June 4, 1919, <www.fordham.edu /halsall/mod//920.womensvote.html> (May 4, 2009).

GLOSSARY

abolitionist—Reformer who wanted to bring about a complete end to slavery.

activist—Person who takes an active role in organizations that work to bring about change.

advocate—Person who defends a cause or individual.

amendment—Change, especially to a legal document such as a constitution.

arsenal—Building where weapons and ammunition are stored.

Bloomer dress—Loose trousers covered by a knee-length skirt.

censure—Express public disapproval.

elitism—Attitude that one's own group or class is superior to others.

emancipation—Granting of freedom.

franchise—A right of citizenship granted to an individual by the government, especially the right to vote.

malaria—Disease carried by mosquitoes, causing severe chills and fever.

mortgage—A loan based on a house or piece of property.

obituary—Written tribute to someone who has died.

opium—Addictive drug with some medical uses.

orator—Public speaker.

petition—Document addressed to legislators, calling for a change in law or policy and signed by supporters.

racism—Belief that one race is superior or that other races are inferior.

radical—Extreme; threatening the established order.

reformer—Person who works to bring about positive change in society.

secede—To withdraw from a group.

self-sovereignty—The capacity to think and act for oneself.

suffrage—The right or privilege of voting.

temperance—The moderate use of alcohol.

tyranny—Government controlled by cruel and powerful leaders.

FURTHER READING

Books

Adams, Colleen. *Women's Suffrage: A Primary Source History of the Women's Rights Movement in America.* New York: Rosen, 2003.

Adiletta, Dawn C. *Elizabeth Cady Stanton: Women's Suffrage and the First Vote.* New York: Rosen/PowerPlus Books, 2005.

Bausum, Ann. *With Courage and Cloth: Winning the Fight for a Woman's Right to Vote.* Washington, D.C.: National Geographic, 2004.

Burgan, Michael. *Elizabeth Cady Stanton: Social Reformer.* Minneapolis, Minn.: Compass Point Books, 2006.

Harness, Cheryl. *Rabble-Rousers: Twenty Women Who Made a Difference.* New York: Dutton Children's Books, 2003.

Moore, Heidi. *Elizabeth Cady Stanton.* Chicago: Heinemann Library, 2004.

Internet Addresses

Elizabeth Cady Stanton House
<http://www.nps.gov/history/nR/travel/pwwmh/ny10.htm>

Not For Ourselves Alone—The Story of Elizabeth Cady Stanton and Susan B. Anthony
<http://www.pbs.org/stantonanthony/>

Open Collections Program: Women Working, 1800–1930—Elizabeth Cady Stanton
<http://ocp.hul.harvard.edu/ww/people_stanton.html>

INDEX